T0365920

DAY-TO-DAY
WITH
*K*imberella
AND *P*rince
Ain't-So-Charmin'

*(Over the Crick
and Through the Sticks
To Buckskins' Cabin We Go!)*

KIMBERLY A. WEIRES

WESTBOW
PRESS®
A DIVISION OF THOMAS NELSON
& ZONDERVAN

WestBow Press books may be ordered through
booksellers or by contacting:

WestBow Press
A Division of Thomas Nelson & Zondervan
1663 Liberty Drive
Bloomington, IN 47403
www.westbowpress.com
844-714-3454

ISBN: 978-1-6642-7036-7 (sc)
ISBN: 978-1-6642-7035-0 (e)

Print information available on the last page.

WestBow Press rev. date: 07/23/2022

Dedication

I would like to thank my personal Savior, Jesus Christ; my husband and best friend on Earth, Rodney; my children, Jacob (Sara) and Julie (Grant); my grandchildren, Mary, Elinor, Isabelle, Cole, Kate and Ryan; family and friends for many wonderful memories and for future ones that will more than likely come.

How to be God's child:

Tell Him that you are sorry for your sins and ask for forgiveness.

Acknowledge that Jesus Christ is God's Son and that He died on the cross for your sins.

Tell Him that you would like to be a child of His and live your life for Him from now on and thank Him for accepting you into His family.

You'll have the Holy Spirit dwelling within you and it is a great feeling to know that you will be loved and protected while living out the rest of your life in this world and throughout Eternity!

Don't forget to dive into God's Word by reading your Bible.

BOOK

OF

JOHN

3:16

🌍 FOR GOD SO LOVED THE WORLD 🌍

THAT HE

GAVE HIS

ONE AND

ONLY SON,

THAT WHO-

EVER BELIEVES

IN HIM SHALL

NOT PERISH

BUT HAVE

ETERNAL LIFE

About the Author

Kimberly Weires and her husband, Rodney, have two married children and six grandchildren. Their half-human dog, Fudgy, is in Heaven now and is more than likely stirring things up.

Weires has previously published five books of devotions in the series *Day-To-Day with Kimberella and Prince Ain't–So–Charmin'*: (If the Shoe Fits...Run!); (Still Havin' a Ball!); (Is It Midnight Yet?!); (MY Prince Was NEVER a Frog!); (My Pumpkin Awaits!...It's About Time)

Cast of Characters

 **Kimberella** – Main character; wife of Prince Roderick; mother to Jack and Jules; grandmother to Mary Lu, Izzy Ann, Lanore, Chew-Chew, Baby No-No and Little Trooper

 **Prince Roderick** – Main character; husband of Kimberella; father to Jack and Jules; grandfather to Mary Lu, Izzy Ann, Lanore, Chew-Chew, Baby No-No and Little Trooper

 Jack – Son of Kimberella and Prince Roderick; husband of Sara-Sara; father to Mary Lu and Lanore; brother to Jules

 Sara-Sara – Daughter-In-Law of Kimberella and Prince Roderick; wife of Jack; mother to Mary Lu and Lanore

 Mary Lu – Granddaughter of Kimberella and Prince Roderick; daughter of Jack and Sara-Sara; big sister to Lanore; cousin to Izzy Ann, Chew-Chew, Baby No-No and Little Trooper

Lanore – Granddaughter of Kimberella and Prince Roderick; daughter of Jack and Sara-Sara; little sister to Mary Lu; cousin to Izzy Ann, Chew-Chew, Baby No-No and Little Trooper

Jules – Daughter of Kimberella and Prince Roderick; wife of The General; mother to Izzy Ann, Chew-Chew, Baby No-No and Little Trooper; sister to Jack

The General – Son-In-Law of Kimberella and Prince Roderick; husband of Jules; father to Izzy Ann, Chew-Chew, Baby No-No and Little Trooper

Izzy Ann – Granddaughter of Kimberella and Prince Roderick; daughter of Jules and The General; big sister to Chew-Chew, Baby No-No and Little Trooper; cousin to Mary Lu and Lanore

Chew-Chew – Grandson of Kimberella and Prince Roderick; son of Jules and The General; little brother to Izzy Ann and big brother to Baby No-No and Little Trooper; cousin to Mary Lu and Lanore

Baby No-No – Granddaughter of Kimberella and Prince Roderick; daughter of Jules and The General; little sister to Izzy Ann and Chew-Chew; big sister to Little Trooper; cousin to Mary Lu and Lanore

Little Trooper – Grandson of Kimberella and Prince Roderick; son of Jules and The General; little brother to Izzy Ann, Chew-Chew and Baby No-No; cousin to Mary Lu and Lanore

Fudgy – Old English Sheepdog; so-called pet of Kimberella and Prince Roderick; master-of-the-cabin; cousin to Witty Kitty; obnoxious, yet adorable

Witty Kitty – Smart cat of no particular breed; Jules' and The General's pet whenever he decides to stop in; cousin to Fudgy; handsome and sassy

📖 **Proverbs 17:6** Children's children are a crown to the aged, and parents are the pride of their children.

❓<u>**Question of the day:** **"As a child of God, are we living our lives in such a way to make Him proud to call us His children?"**</u>

⚱ "I think that going to visit your grandparents in their home or cabin can be a memorable and educational experience!"

✳JANUARY 1✳

⚱ Mary Lu's experience: "If your grandparents happen to live in a cabin out in the country like mine does, then throw the words 'unusual' and 'unpredictable' into the mix."

✝ God's country.

📖 **Proverbs 3:23-24** Then you will go on your way in safety, and your foot will not stumble; when you lie down, you will not be afraid; when you lie down, your sleep will be sweet.

❓Question of the day: "When you lie down to go to sleep, are you afraid or do you just close your eyes and know that God is in control?"

👤 **"As you make your bed every morning after a good night's sleep, don't forget to thank God for another beautiful day!"**

✳JANUARY 2✳

👤 **Baby No–No's advice: "Please remember to count your blessings, which starts with a bed to sleep on."**

✚ **Sweet dreams.**

📖 **P**salm 37:12-13 The wicked plot against the righteous and gnash their teeth at them; but the Lord laughs at the wicked, for He knows their day is coming.

❓Question of the day: "Did you know that God laughs?"

👤 "Laughing is a great stress reliever. Our cabin tries to be a stress-free zone."

✳JANUARY 3✳

👤 Prince Roderick's observation: "Moderation is the key. All laughing and no stress makes getting chores done nearly impossible."

➕ Even God laughs.

📖 **Proverbs 27:2 Let another praise you, and not your own mouth; someone else, and not your own lips.**

❓Question of the day: "Is there something that you're good at and nobody but God knows about it?"

🧍 **"Never toot your own horn. In other words, do not brag about yourself."**

✳JANUARY 4✳

🐱 **Witty Kitty's meow: "Be humble and *if* someone pays you a compliment, say: 'Praise be to God!'"**

✝ **Amen!**

📖 **Proverbs 17:22 A cheerful heart is good medicine, but a crushed spirit dries up the bones.**

❓**Question of the day: "Did you know that if you pretend to be happy, it will become a habit, which will give you a cheerful heart?"**

🧍 **"There is no pouting at the Buckskins' cabin, boat, car or camper. Nobody likes a pouter, not even the one who is doing the pouting."**

✳JANUARY 5✳

🧍 **Lanore's solution: "Try to have so many fun activities to choose from that there is no time *to* pout."**

✚ **Count your blessings instead.**

📖 **P**roverbs 18:24 A man of many companions may come to ruin, but there is a Friend who sticks closer than a brother.

❓Question of the day: "<u>Do you know who that Friend is?</u>"

🚶 "We are having some close friends coming over for a visit this weekend, so please be on your best behavior."

✳JANUARY 6✳

🐕 Fudgy's bark: "Wait! I thought *I* was your closest friend!"

✚ No Fudgy, it is Jesus!

📖 **P**salm 37:4 Delight yourself in the Lord and He will give you the desires of your heart.

?Question of the day: "What are the desires of your heart?"

🧍 "Time for lunch! We are having tomato soup, grilled cheese sandwiches, potato chips, watermelon and ice–cold lemonade. If you eat everything on your paper plate, you may have a brownie and some homemade peach ice cream."

✳JANUARY 7✳

🧍 Chew–Chew's plea: "Can I turn the crank?"

✚ Say 'Please'.

📖 **Revelation 7:13 Then one of the elders asked me, "These in white robes – who are they, and where did they come from?"**

❓**Question of the day: "Did you know that Jesus can wash your sins as white as snow?"**

🧍 **"There are two kinds of people: Those who like to wear robes and those who do not. There is another kind of person who likes to buy others robes for Christmas presents and then stay at their house the following year to see if they are actually being worn."**

✳JANUARY 8✳

🦴 **Little Trooper's calculation: "So...even though I can't count yet, that makes *three* kinds of people."**

✚ **You can *always* count on God!**

📖 **Revelation 1:3 Blessed is the one who reads the words of this prophecy, and blessed are those who hear it and take to heart what is written in it, because the time is near.**

❓Question of the day: "Did you know that you will be blessed by reading the Book of Revelation?"

👤 "Remember – It is *always* a good idea to read your Bible every day to stay in God's Word."

✳JANUARY 9✳

👤 Izzy Ann's news: "The Bible has everything you need to know for living this life and for your life spent in Eternity."

✚ Try reading the Book of Revelation aloud.

📖 **Proverbs 1:7 The fear of the Lord is the beginning of knowledge, but fools despise wisdom and discipline.**

❓Question of the day: "Did you know that you can pray to have wisdom and understanding?"

🧍 "Okay, I am going to teach you how to tie your own shoes: Crisscross the laces and put the end in and pull tightly. Now make a loop and wrap the other shoelace around it and draw the loop through the other one and pull tightly again."

✳JANUARY 10✳

🧍 Baby No-No's question: "Now that Grandpa had his lesson for the day, can he please come out and play with us?"

✚ Great lessons are found in the book of Proverbs.

📖 **Exodus 20:7 "You should not misuse the Name of the Lord your God, for the Lord will not hold anyone guiltless who misuses His Name..."**

?Question of the day: "Can we even imagine how we would feel if someone used our name to express hate?"

👤 **"While outside in cold weather at our cabin, boots with three or more buckles *and* are required to be fitted over your shoes, need to be outlawed."**

❋JANUARY 11❋

👤 **Prince Roderick's opinion: "Sometimes the word 'practical' is misused and so is the Lord's Name when used in vain. *Never* make that mistake."**

✚ **NEVER!**

📖 **1** **Corinthians 10:31 So whether you eat or drink or whatever you do, do it all for the glory of God.**

❓**Question of the day: "Is this something that's hard to do in today's society when so many of us want to give ourselves credit?"**

🚶 **"While Grandpa is taking all of you sledding down the big hill out back, I will be making my famous hot chocolate complete with mini marshmallows. Do you know that if a recipe calls for big marshmallows and you only have mini ones, it will take ten littles to equal one big?"**

✳JANUARY 12✳

🚶 **Chew–Chew's confession: "All I know is that one hundred marshmallows that are big or small, makes my tummy hurt."**

✚ **Practice self–control.**

📖 **Romans** 11:36 **For from Him and through Him and to Him are all things. To Him be the glory Forever! Amen.**

❓**Question of the day: "Is there anything that you can think of that God didn't have a helping hand in?"**

🧍 **"Needlepoint is a great hand–eye coordination project for you to do on this cold day in January. We just need to come up with an idea for the picture to be drawn on the canvas first."**

✳JANUARY 13✳

🧍 **Lanore's suggestion: "How about a cabin in the woods with a heart surrounding it?"**

✝ **God gives us many gifts and we should use them for His glory.**

📖 **Acts 22:16 And now what are you waiting for? Get up, be baptized and wash your sins away, calling on His Name.**

❓Question of the day: "Are you ready to be baptized?"

🧍 **"Okay kids...listen up! Markers are out to get you. If you need a red marker to complete your apple orchard drawing, it will be dried up. However, that *same* red marker will drop onto your favorite white dress that you like to wear to Sunday School and it will make you look like you lost a fight with a strawberry sundae."**

✶JANUARY 14✶

🧍 **Izzy Ann's conclusion: "I think we need to make the switch to colored pencils."**

✚ **Jesus can wash our sins away.**

📖 **Psalm 139:13 For You created my inmost being; You knit me together in my mother's womb.**

❓Question of the day: "How can the Bible be any clearer that a fetus is a baby...a baby that God created for a purpose?"

🧍 **"Did you ever notice that children want to be older than they are and adults desire to be a kid again? No matter how many candles are on *your* cake each birthday, please be content with the age you are that very day."**

JANUARY 15

🧍 **Lanore's thinking: "You are here on Earth at this time for a reason. God knew you and your purpose in this life *before* you were even born. He wants you to be here at this time, so please ask Him what you can do while you're here."**

✚ **And God *still* gave us a chance at life!**

📖 **1 Corinthians 15:33 Do not be misled: "Bad company corrupts good character."**

❓Question of the day: "<u>Are we being corrupted?</u>"

👤 **"A good rule of thumb is this: Mind your manners *or* someone else will mind them for you. Thank you for being polite."**

✳JANUARY 16✳

🐕 **Fudgy's response: "You are very welcome!"**

➕ **Dog spelled backwards is god, with a lower case "g", of course.**

📖 **P**salm 118:22 The stone the builders rejected has become the capstone; the Lord has done this, and it is marvelous in our eyes.

❓Question of the day: "Is Jesus the capstone in your life?"

🧍 "Legos, Lincoln Logs, Tinker Toys and Building Blocks are all considered ideal for children to learn about construction."

✳JANUARY 17✳

🧍 Mary Lu's experience: "The best thing you can build is your relationship with Jesus."

✚ He is our Cornerstone!

📖 **Zechariah 14:20** On that day HOLY TO THE LORD will be inscribed on the bells of the horses, and the cooking pots in the Lord's House will be like the sacred bowls in front of the altar.

❓Question of the day: "Wouldn't it be a different world today if we would inscribe "Holy to the Lord" on things we owned?"

🧍 **"Do any of you hear bells jingling? It must be time for a sleigh ride with Grandpa and his horse, Charlie."**

✳JANUARY 18✳

🐈 **Witty Kitty's warning: "Watch out for sudden stops!"**

✚ **God can even make a donkey talk.**

📖 **P**roverbs 10:19 When words are many, sin is not absent, but he who holds his tongue is wise.

?<u>Question of the day: "Is it just me or do other people have a hard time holding their tongue?"</u>

🕴 "Let's jump rope: "Mommy, Mommy...I feel sick. Call the doctor quick, quick, quick. In comes the doctor, in comes the nurse, in comes the lady with the alligator purse."

✳JANUARY 19✳

✏ Little Trooper's feelings: "I think I'll just be quiet for another year if that's the kind of gibberish they will teach me to say when I decide to talk."

➕ Think *before* talking.

📖 **Hebrews 13:5 Keep your lives free from the love of money and be content with what you have, because God has said, "Never will I leave you; never will I forsake you."**

❓**Question of the day: "Are you content with what you have?"**

🧍 **"At our cabin, the only television we have is hooked up to either a DVD or VHS player. In other words, no cable T.V."**

✳JANUARY 20✳

🧍 **Kimberella's comment: "We have a few totes of exciting documentaries that include: 'The Construction of Hoover Dam'; 'Mule rides into the Grand Canyon'; 'Erection of the St. Louis Arch'; 'Finding Noah's Ark'; and 'Hunting for Bigfoot'. Well...maybe 'hunting' is a bit harsh."**

✚ **Christian book stores and museums have a great selection to choose from.**

📖 **1** **Corinthians 11:2 I praise you for remembering me in everything and for holding to the traditions just as I passed them on to you.**

❓Question of the day: "What traditions do you have?"

🧍 **"At our cabin you don't need to be a cowboy or cowgirl to wear a hat. For that matter, you don't even need to own a horse."**

JANUARY 21

🧍 **Chew–Chew's observation: "Grandpa has a lot of hats, but only one head."**

✚ **Remember to remove your hat during prayer to show your respect to God.**

📖 **Matthew 11:15 He who has ears, let him hear.**

❓**Question of the day: "Do you hear what I hear?"**

👤 **"Baby...it's cold outside! Please remember to put on your earmuffs and Grandma loves you! I said...'GRANDMA LOVES YOU!'"**

✳JANUARY 22✳

👤 **Baby No–No's reply: "I heard you, but you sounded a bit muffled."**

✚ **There is a big difference between 'hearing' and 'listening'.**

📖 **Matthew 6:14-15: For if you forgive men when they sin against you, your Heavenly Father will also forgive you. But if you do not forgive men their sins, your Father will not forgive your sins.**

❓**Question of the day: "Did you know that in the Lord's Prayer when it says to forgive our trespasses as we forgive those who trespass against us, that we're actually asking God to forgive us as we forgive others?" (Fairly or unfairly)**

🧍 **"When you take the step to forgive someone, you need to remember to *never* bring it up again. God erases our sins through Jesus Christ and when we are forgiven, He forgets about it."**

✳JANUARY 23✳

🧍 **Lanore's conclusion: "Whew!"**

✚ **Don't hold a grudge against anyone!**

📖 **R**evelation 22:2 ...down the middle of the great city. On each side of the river stood the tree of life, bearing twelve crops of fruit, yielding its fruit every month. And the leaves of the tree are for the healing of the nations.

❓<u>Question of the day: "Can you image twelve different fruits growing on one tree?"</u>

👤 **"Who would like a peanut butter and jelly sandwich? I have orange marmalade, apple butter and rhubarb to choose from."**

✳ JANUARY 24 ✳

👤 **Izzy Ann's observation: "I hear crickets."**

✚ **The wide variety of fruit that God created is amazing!**

📖 **Psalm 78:18 They willfully put God to the test by demanding the food they craved.**

❓Question of the day: "Do you feel lucky?" (Don't test God!)

👤 **"Since there isn't a bakery around here for miles and miles, I'm going to turn my kitchenette into one. Today's feature will be hot doughnuts. How many would you like?"**

✷JANUARY 25✷

👤 **Mary Lu's response: "How many _are_ there?"**

✚ **Dough–not be greedy.**

Proverbs 12:10 A righteous man cares for the needs of his animal, but the kindest acts of the wicked are cruel.

Question of the day: "Are you kind to your pets or farm animals?"

"Grandpa likes to do his math exercises by totaling up his family members."

- Grandpa + Grandma = 2
- 2 (us) + 2 (children) = 4
- 4 (us) + 2 (in–laws) = 6
- 6 (us) + 6 (grandchildren) = (1 dozen)

JANUARY 26

Witty Kitty's math: "1 cat + 1 hungry stomach + 1 empty food dish = 1 mad cat."

+ Treat your animals kindly!

📖 Isaiah 11:6 The wolf will live with the lamb, the leopard will lie down with the goat, the calf and the lion and the yearling together; and a little child will lead them.

❓Question of the day: "What kind of wild animal would you like to pet when it is transformed into a tame critter?"

🧍 "There is a farm down the road. Shall we go take a look–see at all of the animals that were born last year? I bet they have grown a lot since then."

✳JANUARY 27✳

🐈 Fudgy's thought: "I know the lambs, bunnies and chicks should be ripe...I mean, 'bigger'."

✚ Please look, but don't touch.

📖 **Colossians 1:16 For by Him all things were created: things in Heaven and on Earth, visible and invisible, whether thrones or powers or rulers or authorities; all things were created by Him and for Him.**

❓Question of the day: "Can we say a big 'NO' to Evolution?"

🧍 **"Once you find a fossil, there is no question if something existed or not. The question is: 'How long ago did it exist?'"**

✳JANUARY 28✳

🐈 **Witty Kitty's experience: "It depends on who you ask. A scientist that believes in Evolution or one who believes in Creation."**

✝ **God believes in Creation and that is good enough for us!**

📖 **Romans 8:26 In the same way, the Spirit helps us in our weakness. We do not know what we ought to pray for, but the Spirit Himself intercedes for us with groans that words cannot express.**

❓Question of the day: "Can't find the words to pray? Ask the Holy Spirit to help you."

🚹 **"We all have choices to make, good or bad, throughout our entire lives. When we just use our own free will, we can make some doozies. Let the Holy Spirit guide you into making the best choices at that moment in time."**

✳JANUARY 29✳

🚹 **Lanore's warning: "I was told that a choice I make now could affect me the rest of my life."**

✚ **That's right, kiddo...so be careful!**

📖 **2** **Corinthians 3:17 Now the Lord is the Spirit, and where the Spirit of the Lord is, there is freedom.**

❓**Question of the day: "Do you have the Spirit dwelling inside of you?"**

🧍 **"Everyone needs to figure out what they need to do to keep out of trouble with their parents and out of the principal's office. And let us not forget to stay out of jail."**

JANUARY 30

🐕 **Fudgy's advice: "Better yet, do things that are pleasing to God, so that you don't have to do just 'good enough' to stay out of big trouble."**

✚ **The Holy Spirit is practically begging to help you.**

📖 **1** John 2:16 For everything in the world – the cravings of sinful man, the lust of his eyes and the boasting of what he has and does – comes not from the Father but from the world.

❓**Question of the day: "What things of the world is keeping us from the Father?"**

🧍 "Even our *cabin* has a junk drawer which contains old keys, frayed kite string, old matches, dead batteries, burned out nightlights, kinked phone cords and dried up rubber bands. What do *you* need?"

✳JANUARY 31✳

🧍 Izzy Ann's response: "I need to keep myself from junking up my life with needless things."

✚ Simplify your life.

📖 **2 Timothy 2:5 Similarly, if anyone competes as an athlete, he does not receive the victor's crown unless he competes according to the rules;...**

❓<u>**Question of the day: "Doesn't it sound pretty easy to earn a victor's crown just from playing by the rules?"**</u>

🚹 "If it's your turn to do the dishes, remember that the more you clean off your plate, the less scrubbing there will be at the sink."

♥FEBRUARY 1♥

🚹 Chew–Chew's motto: "If I clean my plate, I get a healthy portion of dessert for my reward. It is kind of like receiving a crown."

✚ We will cast our crowns at Jesus' feet because He is the reason we have them to begin with!

📖 **Matthew 10:30** And even the very hairs of your head are all numbered.

?Question of the day: "Do you know how many hairs are on your head?"

🧍 "Swimming caps are used in large swimming pools to keep your hair from clogging up their drains. Since we don't have a large swimming pool around for miles, we use our caps to put on watermelons growing out back to help them from getting too much sun."

❤FEBRUARY 2❤

🧍 Prince Roderick's gripe: "We don't *need* eighty-five swimming caps *or* that many watermelons!"

✚ God even knows how many melons are in your garden. (Too many)

📖 **Deuteronomy 22:5 A woman must not wear men's clothing, nor a man wear women's clothing, for the Lord your God detests anyone who does this.**

❓**Question of the day: "Do any of us want to do something that is detestable to God?"**

🧍 **"Today let's learn how to sew on a button. Then you can either repair a garment that lost one or replace all of the buttons on an article of clothing just for fun."**

❤FEBRUARY 3❤

🧍 **Mary Lu's hint: "In a sewing department or even from my very own collection of buttons, I have many colors and shapes to choose from that can change the look of my outfit with a flick of a needle."**

✚ **Just make sure your insides are in order.**

James 3:8 ...but no man can tame the tongue. It is a restless evil, full of deadly poison.

?Question of the day: "Did you know that the tongue has so much power over us if we let it?"

"Stickers are fun! You can decorate a folder, a page in your music book after mastering a song, and even stick one on your refrigerator just because."

❤FEBRUARY 4❤

Little Trooper's thought: "The company that makes envelopes needs to figure out what glue they use on stickers and apply it to their product."

✚ Sometimes sealing your lips can be challenging.

📖 **Titus 3:1–2 Remind the people to be subject to rulers and authorities, to be obedient, to be ready to do whatever is good, to slander no one, to be peaceable and considerate, and to show true humility towards all men.**

❓**Question of the day: "Are we ready to be obedient to God?"**

🧍 **"At the cabin, also known as the palace, please say 'please'; 'thank you'; 'you're welcome' and 'excuse me'. Thank you!"**

♥FEBRUARY 5♥

🧍 **Baby No–No's response: "You're welcome, now please excuse me."**

✝ **That about covers it!**

📖 **P**salm 41:3 The Lord will sustain him on his sickbed and restore him from his bed of illness.

❓Question of the day: "Do you want to feel better the next time you come down with something?" (Trust God)

🧍 "It doesn't hurt a thing to have a degree in nursing when you live way out in the sticks like we do. For that matter, being a veterinarian wouldn't be a bad idea either."

❤FEBRUARY 6❤

🐈 Fudgy's confession: "Okay, so I'm a klutz."

✚ Admitting your faults is a step in the right direction...look out!

📖 **Psalm 99:3 Let them praise Your Great and Awesome Name – He is Holy.**

❓**Question of the day: "Isn't it easy to praise a God that is as Awesome as He is?"**

🧍 **"Radios are a great way to entertain or inform the listener. Before the invention of television, they were *the* thing to have. Even today most homes and vehicles contain at least one of these contraptions."**

❤FEBRUARY 7❤

🧴 **Little Trooper's opinion: "I like it when the radio is tuned into a song praising God. It makes me fall asleep for my afternoon nap quickly.....zzzzzzzzzz"**

➕ **Stay tuned.**

📖 **1** **Corinthians 14:40 But everything should be done in a fitting and orderly way.**

❓<u>**Question of the day**</u>: **<u>"Is there something in</u>** · **<u>our lives that could use some tidying up?"</u>**

🧍 **"At our cabin, homework means beating rugs, sweeping the porches, emptying ashes from the wood burner, dusting the logs, baking fresh bread, feeding the chickens and picking up after the animals."**

♥FEBRUARY 8♥

🐈 **Witty Kitty's two cents worth: "Do your homework and do some housekeeping within yourself."**

➕ **Clean up your act if you haven't already done so.**

📖 **Nahum 1:5** The mountains quake before Him and the hills melt away.

❓**Question of the day:** "Did you know that the mountains and hills can react to God like this?"

👤 "We don't have any mountains in our part of the sticks, but our rolling hills really rock!"

♥FEBRUARY 9♥

👤 Mary Lu's idea: "I wish everyone could have their own private mountain to climb so they can feel closer to God."

✝ There must be *something* to it!

📖 John 1:1–2 In the beginning was the Word, and the Word was with God, and the Word was God. He was with God in the beginning.

❓Question of the day: "Did you know that the Word is Jesus Christ and He was with God from the very beginning, even before He was born as a baby in the manger?"

🚶 "Museums are a terrific place to learn about the past. Our cabin is a lot like a museum because we live *way* in the past."

♥FEBRUARY 10♥

🚶 Izzy Ann's lesson: "You can learn from another person's mistake *and* from their successes. You should read your Bible for some of the best examples ever!"

✚ Genesis means 'beginning', which is a good place to start.

📖 **James 3:12 My brothers, can a fig tree bear olives, or a grapevine bear figs? Neither can a salt spring produce fresh water.**

❓**Question of the day: "Are you ready to be the salt in the area where you live?"**

🚹 "At our cabin we have a crick. You can't really swim in it, but wading is an option. One thing is for sure, you won't get a mouthful of salt if you put your head under water."

♥FEBRUARY 11♥

🚹 **Kimberella's question: "Why is it that nobody likes to taste salt in the ocean, however the sales of sea salt to season our food with have sky–rocketed?"**

✚ **Because having ocean water in your mouth is too much like gargling.**

🚹 (Oh...)

📖 **Habakkuk 2:3 For the revelation awaits an appointed time; it speaks of the end and will not prove false. Though it linger, wait for it; it will certainly come and will not delay.**

❓Question of the day: "Are you ready?"

🕺 "An airplane flies over our cabin every hour, day *and* night, since the airport is right over yonder. You can even set your watch to it."

♥FEBRUARY 12♥

🕺 Baby No–No's comment: "*Unless* you hear that Grandma and Grandpa Buckskin are leaving for a vacation, then it will be delayed for an entire day when they go to board it."

✝ God's love is *never* delayed!

📖 **R**omans 5:8 But God demonstrates His love for us in this: While we were still sinners, Christ died for us.

?Question of the day: "Have you asked Jesus to forgive you of your sins?"

🧍 **"God is love...God loves us...God sent Jesus...Jesus died for us...Jesus loves us...We love Jesus...We love God...We ARE blessed!"**

♥FEBRUARY 13♥

🧍 **Chew–Chew's awakening: "That is a lot of love!"**

✚ **The Bible is God's love letter to each one of us.**

📖 John 13:34-35 "A new command I give you: Love one another. As I have loved you, so you must love one another. By this all men will know that you are My disciples, if you love one another."

❓**Question of the day: "Isn't love a wonderful thing?"**

👤 "It is Valentine's Day, so I'm going to fire up the oven and you can all join in the fun of baking and decorating sugar cookies real pretty–like for your kinfolk."

❤FEBRUARY 14❤

👤 Lanore's plea: "Can we please make some fun Valentine cards with you?"

✝ Don't miss the opportunity today to tell someone that you love them!

📖 **Hebrews 4:13 Nothing in all Creation is hidden from God's sight. Everything is uncovered and laid bare before the eyes of Him to Whom we must give account.**

❓**Question of the day: "Isn't this humbling?"**

🧍 **"What makes you smile? For Grandpa it is enjoying a warm piece of cherry pie with a big scoop of vanilla ice cream on top."**

♥FEBRUARY 15♥

✏️ **Little Trooper's observation: "I smile when I see *Grandma* smiling as she spies on Grandpa through the crack in the door, watching him eat her dessert she prepared especially for him."**

✚ **God is always watching...ALWAYS!**

📖 **G**enesis 6:20 Two of every kind of bird, of every kind of animal and of every kind of creature that moves along the ground will come to you to be kept alive.

❓Question of the day: "Did you know that God sent the animals to Noah and he didn't have to round them up?"

🧍 "Noah's ark wasn't designed like the kind you see in children's story books – making it look like a bathtub toy with animals stuffed into it. It was a huge vessel with multiple decks and had plenty of room for all who entered. In other words, built more like a ship."

♥FEBRUARY 16♥

🧍 Prince Roderick's comment: "The animals came to Noah, two by two. I wish Fudgy and Witty Kitty would follow their example when we call them in for supper each evening."

✚ In the last days...scoffers.

📖 **P**salm 144:1 Praise be to the Lord my Rock, who trains my hands for war, my fingers for battle.

❓Question of the day: "Is the Lord your Rock?"

👤 "Do you like the old school desks that have lids that flip up? I do, because I can hide baked goods in there so Grandpa can't find them. It would be the *last* place he would look."

♥FEBRUARY 17♥

👤 Izzy Ann's comment: "Thank you for the tip, Grandma!"

➕ Watch your fingers and don't be a sneak.

📖 **John 14:26 But the Counselor, the Holy Spirit, whom the Father will send in My Name, will teach you all things and will remind you of everything I have said to you.**

❓**Question of the day: "Do you have the Holy Spirit dwelling inside of you?"**

👤 **"Our cabin does not have a drinking fountain, but we do have a bubbling crick. It's definitely more fun!"**

❤FEBRUARY 18❤

👤 **Mary Lu's gripe: "It's hard to get a drink of water without ending up with a mouthful of minnows."**

✚ **Ask the Holy Spirit to fill your cup to overflowing.**

📖 **John 21:12 Jesus said to them, "Come and have breakfast." None of the disciples dared ask Him, "Who are you?" They knew it was the Lord.**

❓**Question of the day: "Do you know that as a believer in Jesus Christ, we will never have to ask Him who He is?"**

🚶 **"Cupcakes are not just for birthday parties anymore. They are enjoyed at weddings, holidays and even for breakfast at our cabin."**

❤FEBRUARY 19❤

🐾 **Fudgy's request: "May I please enjoy three cupcakes tomorrow morning...let's say about 3:15 a.m.? I promise to pray before I devour them."**

✚ **Well, let's hope!**

📖 **Revelation 14:6 Then I saw another angel flying in midair, and he had the Eternal Gospel to proclaim to those who live on the Earth – to every nation, tribe, language and people.**

❓**Question of the day: "If you saw an angel flying in midair, would you question whether or not it is truly an angel?"**

👤 **"Even in our little cabin in the middle of nowhere (a.k.a. the sticks), science can be learned. I use baking soda and vinegar to make a bubbly concoction to unclog the sink's drain."**

❤FEBRUARY 20❤

👤 **Lanore's witnessing: "I've seen Grandpa out in the shed mixing a few things together to remove paint off of the walls inside. Come to think of it, the paint slid plumb off the wall when he tripped over the cans and the substance splattered upwards. It also removes hair."**

✝ **God knows the number of hairs on your head along with approximately 7.5 billion other heads.**

📖 **Proverbs 19:21 Many are the plans in a man's heart, but it is the Lord's purpose that prevails.**

❓**Question of the day: "How many times do we make plans and then they end up changing?"**

🚶 "Put on your best clothes and a coat, because we are going to the city to do some marketing. We can walk on sidewalks and visit an old–fashioned candy shop."

❤FEBRUARY 21❤

🚶 Prince Roderick's bribe: "Or you can stay back at the cabin with me and search for arrowheads in the crick and pick some delicious red and black raspberries."

✚ Remember to say, "The Lord willing" when speaking about your plans.

📖 **Colossians 3:17 And whatever you do, whether in word or deed, do it all in the Name of the Lord Jesus, giving thanks to God the Father through Him.**

❓Question of the day: "Have you thanked God today in Jesus' Name?"

👤 **"God created *all* things. Now please go to sleep and I will make a big breakfast for *all* of you right after the sun rises."**

♥FEBRUARY 22♥

👤 **Chew–Chew's dream: "God made the chickens that lay eggs, the kind of trees that have syrup in them, pigs made out of pork and bushes that grow berries on them. Thank you God for feeding us!"**

✚ **You are welcome!**

📖 **1 Corinthians 6:19–20: Do you not know that your body is a temple of the Holy Spirit, who is in you, whom you have received from God? You are not your own; you were bought for a price. Therefore honor God with your body.**

❓**Question of the day: "This kind of makes you think, doesn't it?"**

👤 **"When your body craves something it is said that the reason for it is due to a lack of a particular element (i.e.: salt, sugar, vitamins, minerals, fiber, starch, etc.)"**

❤**FEBRUARY 23**❤

👤 **Baby No–No's question: "What does Grandpa need when he is eating a hot fudge sundae with whipped cream, cherries, nuts, bananas and toasted coconut on it?"**

✚ **A diet.**

📖 **Matthew 5:48 Be perfect, therefore, as your Heavenly Father is perfect.**

❓**Question of the day: "Do you know that we will never be perfect, but we should aim for it the best we can?"**

👤 **"Gloves come in handy when you are working outside and it is too cold to do the chore without them. The problem is that all of your fingers and thumbs are separated from each other and they get colder faster than if you wore mittens."**

♥FEBRUARY 24♥

👤 **Lanore's solution: "Save the chore until spring and wear mittens to build a snowman instead."**

✚ **A snowman may be without sin – but only Jesus is perfect.**

📖 **Mark 8:25 Once more Jesus put His hands on the man's eyes. Then his eyes were opened, his sight was restored, and he saw everything clearly.**

❓**Question of the day: "Did you know that if you have the Holy Spirit dwelling inside of you, you will be able to see things more clearly?"**

🧍 **"'Grandpa, do you know where my glasses are?' 'They're on top of your head.' 'Ok, funny man, where are *your* glasses?' 'On my face!' 'I better go to town and get a stronger prescription.'"**

❤FEBRUARY 25❤

🧍 **Mary Lu's eyewitness account: "No matter how much your eyes can see or *not* see, just make sure they are wide open to see things like Jesus does."**

✝ **Amen!**

📖 **Acts 13:9 Then Saul, who was also called Paul, filled with the Holy Spirit, looked straight at Elymas and said, "You are a child of the devil and an enemy of everything that is right! You are full of all kinds of deceit and trickery. Will you never stop perverting the right way of the Lord?..."**

❓Question of the day: "Shouldn't we all try to be a 'Paul' and not a 'Saul'?"

👤 **"The store for the big & tall, the short & small at the mall that has it all, will be closing this fall. Instead of using the building for a hall to have a ball, a farmer had the gall to tear it down and build a stall."**

❤FEBRUARY 26❤

👤 **Izzy Ann's statement: "Good call."**

✚ **Did you know that in the Bible Saul became Paul?**

📖 **M**atthew 15:26 He replied, "It is not right to take the children's bread and toss it to their dogs."

❓**Question of the day: "Did you know that Jesus is the Bread of Life?"**

🧍 "It's my nap time, so please play outside of the cabin (except for the babies.)"

❤FEBRUARY 27❤

🐕 Fudgy's question: "Am I a baby? Grandma calls me that as a nickname. Then again, Grandpa calls me a few things that I'm not, so I guess I'll join the big kids outdoors."

➕ Please don't call people (or dogs) names!

📖 **E**phesians 5:4 Nor should there be obscenity, foolish talk or coarse joking, which are out of place, but rather thanksgiving.

❓**Question of the day: "If you hear someone telling an inappropriate joke, are you willing to walk away from it?"**

👤 "Jokes *can* be funny, but they *must* be clean at our cabin. In fact, don't tell one to your Grandparents that you wouldn't utter if God was in the room."

♥FEBRUARY 28♥

👤 Baby No–No's joke: "What has ears, but can't hear? The answer is: 'Grandpa'. You probably thought it was 'corn', right?"

✚ God is *always* in the room and that's no joke!

📖 **M**ark 9:1 And He said to them, "Truly I tell you, some who are standing here will not taste death before they see that the Kingdom of God has come with power."

❓Question of the day: "Are you looking up?"

🚹 "Well, I can see by looking out my kitchen window, that enough snow fell last night so all of you kiddies can make a snowman, snow fort or an entire village made of the white stuff. Let's get your snow pants on."

❤FEBRUARY 29❤

🐱 Witty Kitty's glee: "Another day spent in front of the fireplace toasting marshmallows. What a life. Thank you God for *all* of my nine lives."

✝ I hate to tell you this, but cats only have only one life to live like the rest of God's Creation.

📖 **Genesis 18:14 Let a little water be brought, and then you may all wash your feet and rest under this tree.**

❓**Question of the day: "Do you take time to rest?"**

🚹 **"An alarm clock can be a useful gadget to make sure you wake up in time, however, out in the sticks you may wake up to roosters crowing, cows mooing and Grandpa cooking bacon over an open fire before the thing even goes off."**

🐿️ MARCH 1 🐿️

✏️ **Little Trooper's two cents worth:** *"Or* if I decide to cry for my 5:00 a.m. feeding."

✝️ **God's timing is perfect.**

📖 **P**roverbs 21:25 The craving of a sluggard will be the death of him, because his hands refuses to work.

❓Question of the day: "Do you know that the Bible says that if you don't work, you won't eat?" (2 Thessalonians 3:10)

👤 "How long does it take to put dirty clothes into a hamper after wearing them? Apparently in some cases about 4 – 5 days."

🐎 MARCH 2 🐎

👤 Kimberella's plea: "Please don't be that person!"

✚ If something is dirty, clean it up. If it's too dirty to get clean, either get rid of it or use it as a rag to clean something else up.

📖 **Genesis 32:25** When the man saw that he could not overpower him, he touched the socket of Jacob's hip so that his hip was wrenched as he wrestled with the man.

?Question of the day: "What are you wrestling with today?"

👤 "If I am trying to show you how to use a hula hoop, please don't laugh. If Grandpa is the one spinning it on his hips...stand back!"

🎋 MARCH 3 🎋

👤 Chew–Chew's advice: "Stand back a little more."

✚ Be hip...find Jesus!

📖 **Romans 12:4–5 For just as each of us has one body with many members, and these members do not all have the same function, in Christ we though many, form one body, and each member belongs to all the others.**

❓**Question of the day: "What function do you have that will blend in with the other members?"**

👤 **"A bus can haul you and your family around the city to see the sights. Grandpa's hay wagon can haul the same people around the fields to see the animals."**

🌿 MARCH 4 🌿

👤 **Mary Lu's memory: "I remember when I was three years old and we took the wagon to the little country church's annual picnic. It was great fun!"**

✝ **It don't get no better than that!**

📖 **P**roverbs 3:5–6 Trust in the Lord with all your heart and lean not on your own understanding; in all your ways acknowledge Him, and He will make your paths straight.

❓<u>Question of the day</u>: "Isn't it nice to be able to depend on the Lord to lead us down the right path?"

👤 "I sure could use a potholder in my kitchenette for handling all of those hot dishes. I also know that Grandpa needs one or two of them outside for his cookouts. Now, let's see here...who did we give that loom kit to last Christmas?"

🎋 MARCH 5 🎋

👤 Chew–Chew's confession: "I don't have time to weave potholders, because mommy needs me to make a patchwork quilt for the baby. Can I please put in a request for a toy truck for this Christmas? It is more up my alley."

➕ Don't weave aimlessly through your life – take the straight path.

📖 **G**enesis 11:6 The Lord said, "If as one people speaking the same language they have begun to do this, then nothing they plan to do will be impossible for them..."

❓Question of the day: "Do you know that in today's world we can have our different languages translated through our computers, thus giving everyone the ability to speak the same language?"

🚹 "Before the invention of the computer, little girls would spend hours cutting out paper dolls' clothing. Now they can spend hours searching the internet looking for the perfect paper doll."

🎀MARCH 6🎀

🚹 Izzy Ann's reality: "There isn't any internet at my grandparent's cabin, so I better go find the scissors."

✚ Please use your computer in moderation.

📖 **1** **Peter 2:7 Now to you who believe, this stone is precious. But to those who do not believe, "The stone the builders rejected has become the capstone....**

❓<u>**Question of the day**</u>: <u>**"Are you a believer or a nonbeliever?"**</u>

👤 **"Please remember that respect is a two-way street. No matter what age you are and the other person is, be considerate. Thank you!"**

🐎 MARCH 7 🐎

🐈 **Witty Kitty's fit: "That goes for dogs, too."**

✚ **Please be respectful of God's Commandments.**

📖 **P**roverbs 27:4 Anger is cruel and fury overwhelming, but who can stand before jealousy?

?Question of the day: "Does it make sense that God doesn't want us jealous of each other, since Satan is jealous of God?"

👤 **"Do you ever wonder why the other kids are all pointing at you and whispering? It's because the hat I knitted for you has a bunny face on the back of it. They are just jealous."**

❧**MARCH 8**❧

👤 **Lanore's warning: "God does not like jealously. That is why the evil one has a huge problem."**

✚ **Be thankful for what you *do* have.**

📖 **P**roverbs 12:10 A righteous man cares for the needs of his animal, but the kindest acts of the wicked are cruel.

❓Question of the day: "Are you kind to your pet?"

🧍 "The Veterinarian is paying us a visit to check on Charlie Horse, the chickens, goats, Witty Kitty, Fudgy and to give us humans a Tetanus shot. Hopefully, there will be no evidence of foaming at the mouth."

🌿 MARCH 9 🌿

🧍 Prince Roderick's prediction: *"That* will happen at the viewing of the Vet's bill when it arrives in our mailbox."

✚ Take good care of your animals!

📖 **1 Corinthians 14:15 So what shall I do? I will pray with my spirit, but I will also pray with my mind; I will sing with my spirit, but I will also sing with my mind.**

❓**Question of the day: "Does humming count on this one?"**

🧍 **"The Bible mentions singing numerous times in Heaven. The Book of Psalms is a collection of songs. Can you sing? Do you like to sing? I have a feeling that everyone in Heaven will be able to and have a strong desire to sing praises to God using the voices He will give us."**

⁕ MARCH 10 ⁕

🧍 **Baby No–No's audition: "The wheels on the bus go 'round and 'round..."**

✝ **There are no buses in Heaven, therefore that song will have no meaning.**

📖 **R**evelation 21:4 "...He will wipe every tear from their eyes. There will be no more death or mourning or crying or pain, for the old order of things has passed away."

❓**Question of the day: "Does it get any better than that?"**

🧍 "Some people cry when they are happy, some when they are sad. Some people cry when they are tired, some when they are mad. If you know someone who *never* cries, don't let them fool you."

🎋 MARCH 11 🎋

🔖 Little Trooper's response: "This is where I am an expert!"

✚ There will be no crying in Heaven!

📖 **R**evelation 13:18 This calls for wisdom, if anyone has insight, let him calculate the number of the beast, for it is man's number. His number is 666.

❓**Question of the day: "Do you know if add up the Roman numerals 'D' = 500; 'C' = 100; 'L' = 50; 'X' = 10; 'V' = 5 and 'I' = 1 (The answer will be 666)?"**

🚶 "If you hear a train a–comin' towards the cabin, you better run! It must have derailed about a 1/8 of a mile that–a–way."

🐎 MARCH 12 🐎

🐈 Fudgy's suggestion: "Let's all go count the train cars. It will be a lot easier from the ditch when it whizzes by...1, 2, 3, 4...90, 91, 92..."

✚ Make sure you are on the right track.

📖 **S**ong of Solomon 6:11 I went down to the grove of nut trees to look at the new growth in the valley, to see if the vines had budded or the pomegranates were in bloom.

?Question of the day: "When is the last time you took a nice long walk among God's beautiful Creation?"

🚹 "If you have a tire swing on your property (who doesn't?), you better have a river and vise–versa."

🎺MARCH 13🎺

🚹 Kimberella's comparison: "Kind of like having an apple on a stick – there *better* be a stream of caramel nearby...*please.*"

✚ Would you also like a nut tree?

📖 **Job 40:15 "Look at the behemoth, which I made along with you and which feeds on grass like an ox."**

?Question of the day: "Do you know that the behemoth was more than likely a dinosaur that was created along with man?"

🚹 **"The library is about an hour from our cabin, but the Book Mobile's stop is only fifteen minutes away. Let's all go see if we can find a book or two to read on this rainy day."**

❧ MARCH 14 ❧

🚹 **Chew–Chew's wish: "I hope they have a book on sightings of dinosaurs such as the Loch Ness Monster!"**

✚ **Behemoth that is mentioned in the Bible is another word for dinosaur.**

📖 **1 John 1:9 If we confess our sins, He is faithful and just and will forgive us our sins and purify us from all unrighteousness.**

❓Question of the day: "Isn't this the best news EVER?"

👤 **"Sippy cups have saved many carpets from getting stained by all sorts of sticky, colorful liquids. Grandpa has an adult–sized sippy cup for his coffee, but its main purpose is to keep his mouth from getting burned."**

✄MARCH 15✄

👤 **Baby No–No's secret: "I heard Grandma tell her friend that it is so Grandpa doesn't stain the recliner, couch and rocking chair."**

✚ **Try to keep your soul from getting stained.**

📖 **1 Corinthians 3:7 So neither he who plants nor he who waters is anything, but only God, who makes things grow.**

❓**Question of the day: "Are you willing to depend on God to help you with anything that you attempt in life?"**

🧍 **"Planting a garden can be very rewarding. It can also help teach you patience when waiting for the vegetables to make their appearances. Just don't trip over the squash and melons that are hidden under the...OUCH!"**

🐾 MARCH 16 🐾

🐕 **Fudgy's shout: "Let's play ball!"**

✚ **The Garden of Eden *was* a perfect place.**

📖 **Proverbs 18:13 He who answers before listening – that is his folly and his shame.**

❓Question of the day: "Are we listening to what God is trying to tell us each day?"

👤 "God's gift of life is very important to each one of us, so please buckle up yourselves, small children, toddlers and infants. When Grandpa and I were younger, we didn't wear seat belts."

✺ MARCH 17 ✺

🍼 Little Trooper's thought: "That explains a lot."

✚ Quiet in the back!

📖 **P**roverbs 3:24 ...when you lie down, you will not be afraid; when you lie down, your sleep will be sweet.

❓Question of the day: "Are you ready for some sweet dreams tonight?"

🚹 "Since the drive–in movie theater is about a half hour drive from our cabin, we will just let Grandpa use the side of the barn to project his movie reels on. Tonight's show is 'The Little Rascals'"

🎋**MARCH 18**🎋

🚹 Lanore's question: "I wonder what made him choose *that* one?"

✚ Pleasant dreams!

📖 **Genesis 2:15 The Lord God took the man and put him in the Garden of Eden to work it and take care of it.**

❓Question of the day: "Are we all willing to do the job God wants us to do on this Earth?"

👤 **"Spring is a beautiful season. The grass, trees, bushes and other various plants all come up and out in different shades of green. Then comes rhubarb, morels, flowers and berries. I gotta go to the store and spend some green on mulch, wires and canning jars!"**

🌿MARCH 19🌿

👤 **Mary Lu's reminder: "Don't forget to thank God for everything He created!"**

✚ **Thank you, God!**

📖 **3 John 1:2 Dear friend, I pray that you may enjoy good health and that all may go well with you, even as your soul is getting along well.**

❓<u>**Question of the day: "How is your soul doing lately?"**</u>

🧍 **"Hopefully, no one will need to go to the hospital today or *any* day while playing at our cabin, but if they do, it will be quicker to have Grandpa fire up the hay wagon than to spend fifteen minutes on the phone trying to explain to the person on the other end how to get to our place in the sticks."**

🎉 **MARCH 20** 🎉

🧍 **Izzy Ann's tip: "You can always pray while waiting."**

✚ **Please Lord, keep us all healthy and safe.**

📖 **Colossians 1:16 For by Him all things were created: things in Heaven and on Earth, visible and invisible, whether thrones or powers or rulers or authorities; all things were created by Him and for Him.**

❓**Question of the day: "This sums it up for me...how about you?"**

🧍 **"Evolution teaches us that we came from monkeys. God says in His Holy Word (a.k.a. the Bible) that we came from dirt that He also created. He then breathed life into Adam and created Eve. So...are you going to believe God is the Creator of everything or a text book written by one or more humans (that were created by God) whether or not they realize it?"**

🐾MARCH 21🐾

🐱 **Witty Kitty's statement: "I'll believe in God *and* I believe it is time to feed me."**

✝ **A Designer only make sense.**

📖 **J**ohn 4:13–14 Jesus answered, "Everyone who drinks this water will be thirsty again, but whoever drinks the water I give him will never thirst. Indeed, the water I give him will become in him a spring of water welling up to Eternal Life."

❓**Question of the day: "Are you thirsty?"**

👤 **"Let's have a nice cool drink on the back porch during this unusually warm spring day. Would you like some apple juice, lemonade, iced tea, Kool-Aid, soda pop or just plain water?"**

❧ **MARCH 22** ❧

👤 **Kimberella's motto: "Water is the best drink in the house or outdoors."**

✚ **Everything mentioned above is made with water.**

📖 **Colossians 4:14 Our dear friend Luke, the doctor, and Demas send greetings.**

❓**Question of the day: "Did you know that Luke was a doctor?"**

🚶 **"Let's go outside to jump rope! 'Mommy, Mommy, I feel sick – call the doctor quick, quick, quick – in comes the doctor – in comes the nurse – in comes the lady with the alligator purse.'"**

🎋 MARCH 23 🎋

🚶 **Lanore's beef: "How sick can she or he be? They are j-u-m-p-i-n-g!"**

➕ **Try making exercise fun.**

📖 **1 John 3:19–20 This then is how we know that we belong to the truth, and how we set our hearts at rest in His presence whenever our hearts condemn us. For God is greater than our hearts, and He knows everything.**

?Question of the day: "Is God greater than us?" (Of course He is!)

🧍 **"If you happen to scrape your knee, ankle, elbows, chin or ear (*don't ask*), Grandma has the right bandage for you."**

🐿️MARCH 24🐿️

🧍 **Chew–Chew's concern: "I hope that you are not out of crutches."**

✚ **God doesn't *need* to ask, because He already knows.**

📖 **R**omans 8:26 **In the same way, the Spirit helps us in our weakness. We do not know what we ought to pray for, but the Spirit Himself intercedes for us with groans that words cannot express.**

?Question of the day: "Isn't it great to know that we can pray anytime we want to, because the Holy Spirit has our back?"

👤 "At our cabin out in the sticks, we have bucket swings, horsey swings, regular swings, a porch swing and even a tire swing. Whichever one you choose, just shut your eyes and have a talk with God while you enjoy swinging in the fresh air."

🌿 MARCH 25 🌿

🍼 Little Trooper's hope: "Please let there be a baby swing so I can shut my eyes, too!"

✚ You can talk to God with your eyes open.

📖 **1 Timothy 5:17 The elders who direct the affairs of the church well are worthy of double honor, especially those whose work is preaching and teaching.**

❓Question of the day: "Are you able to be an elder of your church?"

🧍 **"Please always respect your elders. You don't have to agree with everything they say, but respect them. Thank you! (The Management)"**

🎋 MARCH 26 🎋

🐈 **Fudgy's response: "I get the drift."**

✚ **If your elders know more than you do, imagine what God knows!**

📖 **P**roverbs 7:23 ...till an arrow pierces his liver, like a bird darting into a snare, little knowing it will cost him his life.

?Question of the day: "Do you know that you don't have to lose your life if you have Jesus Christ as your Savior?" (You will have Eternal Life)

🧍 "The kiddies were screaming as they came barreling inside the kitchenette the other day. They supposedly saw a big black spider and the web it was spinning inside the shed out back. I tried to tell them that the web is used to trap other annoying insects that either walks or flies into it."

🕷MARCH 27🕷

🧍 Mary Lu's analysis: "Kind of like the 'world wide web'...now *that's* scary!"

✚ Don't get trapped!

📖 **2** Corinthians 9:7 Each man should give what he has decided in his heart to give, not reluctantly or under compulsion, for God loves a cheerful giver.

?Question of the day: "Are you cheerful when you give a gift?"

🧍 "Everyone should learn how to count money in case you have a job in the future that requires it."

🎀 MARCH 28 🎀

🧍 Izzy Ann's tip: "Please remember that it is God's money and that He gave you the ability to earn it."

✚ Be good stewards.

📖 **Mark 1:35 Very early in the morning, while it was still dark, Jesus got up, left the house and went off to a solitary place, where He prayed.**

❓**Question of the day: "Do you have a specific place that is quiet to do your praying?"**

🧍 **"Worms are plentiful in the ground, all around the cabin and other buildings. There are enough for the birds, raccoons *and* to go fishing bright and early tomorrow morning."**

🌿MARCH 29🌿

🧍 **Prince Roderick's question: "How much sleep will I get between midnight and bright and early?"**

✚ **Enough.**

🧍 **(Oh...)**

📖 **Zechariah 8:5** "...so now I have determined to do good again to Jerusalem and Judah. Do not be afraid..."

❓**Question of the day: "What are you afraid of?"**

👤 **"Which board game would you like to play? Grandpa always complains that he's not 'bored' enough whenever I ask him."**

🎆**MARCH 30**🎆

👤 **Baby No–No's request: "Can we please play Hi–Ho Cherrio?"**

✚ **Probably not...it took two nurses and a doctor to take a cherry out of your nose last time you played that game.**

📖 **R**evelation 21:18–21 The wall was made of jasper, and the city of pure gold, as pure as glass. The foundations of the city walls were decorated with every kind of precious stone. The first foundation was jasper, the second sapphire, the third chalcedony, the fourth emerald, the fifth sardonyx, the sixth carnelian, the seventh chrysolite, the eighth beryl, the ninth topaz, the tenth turquoise, the eleventh jacinth, and the twelfth amethyst. The twelve gates were twelve pearls, each gate made of a single pearl. The great street of the city as of pure gold, like transparent glass.

❓Question of the day: "Don't you think that this could be the most beautiful place we have ever seen?"

👤 "Let's plant some flowers all around our cabin. We can either start with seeds or buy some plants that are already in pots. It's great fun to select colors that match your house or cabin."

🌸MARCH 31🌸

👤 Izzy Ann's imagination: "I wonder if flowers come in dark brown?"

✚ In Heaven we may be able to see colors we didn't even know existed!

📖 **When Jesus spoke again to the people, He said, "I am the Light of the world. Whoever follows Me will never walk in darkness, but will have the light of life."**

❓**Question of the day: "Do you know that in Heaven there is no need for the sun and moon?"**

🧍 **"An umbrella is very useful for keeping yourself from getting soaked through to your skin. Luckily, we keep umbrellas in each of our vehicles in case a rain shower pops up. The clouds are looking pretty dark right now, so we better go to town before they break loose."**

⛈APRIL 1⛈

🐱 **Witty Kitty's prank: "April Fool's!"**

✚ **Jesus is always our light even on a gloomy day!**

📖 **E**phesians 6:1 Children, obey your parents in the Lord, for this is right.

❓**Question of the day: "Are we obeying our parents no matter what age we are today?"**

🧍 "If you hang up your clothes they will be wrinkle free. If you don't hang up your clothes, you will cause wrinkles on your parents' faces."

☔APRIL 2☔

🧍 Lanore's advice: "When in doubt, avoid a shout."

✚ Please obey your parents and respect your elders.

📖 **Genesis 6:15 This is how you are to build it: The ark is to be 450 feet long, 75 feet wide and 45 feet high.**

❓Question of the day: "Did you happen to visit the Ark Encounter yet?"

🧍 **"Puddles can be very large out in the country. Some may even be big enough for you to float in (now that's big!)"**

☔APRIL 3☔

🧍 **Kimberella's curiosity: "How can a huge ship like the Titanic float, yet even the smallest of stones will sink when placed in water?"**

✚ **The ark was designed to be a ship not a tubby toy and the Titanic DID sink.**

🧍 **(Oh...)**

📖 **John 6:12 When they all had enough to eat, He said to His disciples, "Gather the pieces that are left over. Let nothing be wasted."**

❓**Question of the day: "Are we eating our leftovers or throwing them away?"**

🧍 **"Springtime at the cabin means dandelion time! Since we don't have any close neighbors, we just let the yellow weeds grow wild. My favorite time is when the dandelions are done being yellow and I can shake them in the air to watch them blow apart."**

🌧APRIL 4🌧

🐈 **Fudgy's thought: "All I see is a bunch of stems just waiting to be turned into necklaces, bracelets and rings by the kiddies."**

✚ **Recycling at its best!**

📖 **James 1:5 If any of you lacks wisdom, he should ask God, who gives generously to all without finding fault, and it will be given to him.**

❓Question of the day: "Have you asked for wisdom lately?"

🧍 "Have you ever made a latch hook rug? They are a super fun project to have *laying* around."

☔APRIL 5☔

🧍 Mary Lu's warning: "Be careful or you could get hooked!"

✚ If you want to be a wise guy – pray for wisdom.

📖 **Matthew 12:33 "Make a tree good and its fruit will be good, or make a tree bad and its fruit will be bad, for a tree is recognized by its fruit."**

?Question of the day: "Are you ready to produce fruit for God?"

🧍 **"I made a basket at my friend's house to hold freshly picked apples. I ended up using it as a centerpiece on the dining room's table."**

☂APRIL 6☂

🧍 **Chew–Chew's dismay: "I wish Grandma would put candy in it like she used to."**

✚ **Fruit is God's candy that's loaded with natural sugar!**

📖 **Proverbs 14:16 A wise man fears the Lord and shuns evil, but a fool is hotheaded and reckless.**

❓Question of the day: "Do you know someone who is hotheaded?"

🧍 **"Grandpa has a couple of lockers he purchased at an auction last week that were locked. He told me he's going out to his shed to find a saw."**

🌧APRIL 7🌧

🧍 **Prince Roderick's attempt: "Let's see here...9 to the left, 1 to the right, 1 to the left...**

✚ **Please watch over him, Lord!**

📖 **1 Corinthians 15:33 Do not be misled: "Bad company corrupts good character."**

❓**Question of the day: "Is it time to evaluate who we hang around with?"**

🧍 **"Let's play Kings' Corners. I'll let you shuffle the cards. Wait! I'll go get my nifty card shuffler that *my* Grandma gave to me for a birthday present many moons ago."**

☔APRIL 8☔

🍼 **Little Trooper's warning: "Please be careful not to get yourself shuffled into the wrong crowd, no matter *what* age you are."**

➕ **Play the cards that you are dealt in life very carefully!**

📖 **Hebrews 11:3 By faith we understand that the universe was formed at God's command, so that what is seen was not made out of what was visible.**

❓**Question of the day: "Do you know that it takes faith to believe in Creation, but it takes even more faith to believe in Evolution?"**

👤 **"Marbles are used in all sorts of games. Some you roll, some you move around a board and some come tumbling down with a loud crash."**

☔APRIL 9☔

👤 **Baby No–No's observation: "To keep yourself from losing *your* marbles, keep in God's Word so when you roll, move and even tumble, He will help *you* get through your day."**

✝ **Maybe the things of the universe are like colorful marbles to God who created them.**

📖 **2** Timothy 3:16–17 All Scripture is God–breathed and is useful for teaching, rebuking, correcting and training in righteousness, so that the man of God may be thoroughly equipped for every good work.

❓**Question of the day: "Do you think about the fact that the Bible is God-breathed as you read it?"**

👤 "Teeter totter, bread and water – wash your face with dirty water. Ok, this see–saw ditty doesn't really rhyme or make any sense, so why is it stuck in my mind after all these years?"

☂APRIL 10☂

👤 Prince Roderick's theory: "Because you taught your children it years ago, who have since taught your grandchildren and so you hear it through the kitchenette's window at least once a week, *that's* why." "Oh..."

✚ Try to memorize Bible verses so they will be available when you need them.

📖 **2 Corinthians 5:17 Therefore, if anyone is in Christ, he is a new creation; the old has gone, the new has come!**

?Question of the day: "Isn't this amazing?"

🧍 **"Today would be a perfect day for Grandpa to get the butterfly net down from the shed's rafters."**

☔APRIL 11☔

🧍 **Izzy Ann's idea: "The perfect place to use the net could be behind the shed among the weeds, because I saw a bunch of caterpillars around there a while ago. I'm glad that God thought of turning those fuzzy crawling things into colorful flying pieces of art!"**

✚ **Someday we may be like butterflies!**

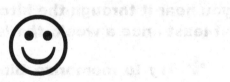

📖 **1** **Thessalonians 4:14 We believe that Jesus died and rose again and so we believe that God will bring with Jesus those who have fallen asleep in Him.**

?Question of the day: "Do you believe in the resurrection?"

ᛁ "Easter is the time of year when we celebrate Jesus' resurrection from death. He is now seated at the Right Hand of God in Heaven."

☂APRIL 12☂

ᛁ Mary Lu's suggestion: "We should all get in the habit of calling it 'Resurrection Sunday', since the word 'Easter' is from a pagan origin."

✝ **Amen!**

📖 **2 Timothy 1:3** I thank God, whom I serve, as my forefathers did, with a clear conscience, as night and day I constantly remember you in my prayers.

❓Question of the day: "Do you remember others in your prayers?"

 "At our cabin we try to show God our gratitude when He answers our prayers – for another day to do His will, our blessings and our relationship with Him through His Son, Jesus Christ."

☂APRIL 13☂

🔖 **Little Trooper's contribution: "Thank you God for our family!"**

✚ **Amen!**

📖 **D**euteronomy 6:7 Impress them in your children. Talk about them when you sit at home and when you walk along the road, when you lie down and when you get up.

?Question of the day: "What things do we impress upon our children?"

👤 "We tried to home school our grandchildren for a few weeks last spring, but all of us contracted Spring Fever and we were shut down."

☂APRIL 14☂

🐱 Witty Kitty's correction: "I believe the word you are looking for is... 'Quarantined'.

✚ Teach the Bible to the young ones in your home...you'll be glad you did.

📖 **Isaiah 41:10 So do not fear, for I am with you; do not be dismayed, for I am your God. I will uphold you with My righteous Right Hand.**

❓Question of the day: "What are you afraid of that God can't handle?"

👤 **"Training wheels turns a big bike into a tricycle–like contraption. They will also keep you from looking like a poster child for a bandage company."**

🌧APRIL 15🌧

👤 **Chew–Chew's plea: "I'm ready to take the risk – can *someone* please take these things off? I'm a big boy now."**

✚ **Don't be crying if you tip over then.**

📖 **1 John 3:4 Everyone who sins breaks the law; in fact, sin is lawlessness.**

?Question of the day: "Don't you think that this is the problem in our world today?"

👤 **"Dancing is great fun in our cabin's barn. Grandpa calls out the dance moves and I play the accordion. The children can promenade until the cows come home."**

☔APRIL 16☔

👤 **Lanore's memory: "Or until the rooster crows...or the people in the black and white cars show up."**

✚ **Obey the law!**

📖 **P**salm 119:18 Open my eyes that I may see wonderful things in Your Law.

❓Question of the day: "Do you pray to have God open your eyes?"

🧍 "My favorite color is...all colors. God created the colors to make flowers, animals, birds, sea life, plants, food and many, many more things. What is *your* favorite color?"

🌧APRIL 17🌧

🐕 Fudgy's yelp: "You're asking me? I'm color blind!"

✚ They now have special glasses that can help with color blindness!

📖 **Matthew 23:4 They tie up heavy loads and put them on men's shoulders, but they themselves are not willing to lift a finger to move them.**

❓Question of the day: "How often do we ask others to do something that we are not willing to do?"

👤 "Tether ball is excellent for strengthening your upper arms and for hand–eye coordination. Whatever you do, don't look over your shoulder if you hear the dinner bell ringing."

☂APRIL 18☂

👤 Izzy Ann's question: "What did you say?!"

✚ Ouch...that HAD to hurt!

📖 **P**roverbs 17:6 Children's children are a crown to the aged, and parents are the pride of their children.

?Question of the day: "Are our children proud of us?"

🧍 "A babysitter makes sure the children are happy, entertained, fed, well-rested, safe and getting along with others."

☂APRIL 19☂

🧍 Lanore's deduction: "It sounds like Grandma and Grandpa to me."

✚ Such a blessing!

📖 **James 1:2–3 Consider it pure joy, my brothers, whenever you face trials of many kinds, because you know that the testing of your faith develops perseverance.**

❓**Question of the day: "Do you view a trial as something that is joyful?"**

🧍 "Since it is raining this morning, let's all go to the new shark exhibit at the Aquarium that is about an hour away from here. You kids can go see the sharks and Grandpa and I will go watch the two minute documentary on underwater photography."

☂APRIL 20☂

🧍 Kimberella's fact: "God knew what He was doing by blessing the shark with so many teeth. Too bad the guy in the diving suit didn't watch the film before he took the plunge."

✚ Test the waters, but please don't test God.

📖 **Song of Solomon 4:2 Your teeth are like a flock of sheep just shorn, coming up from the washing. Each has its twin; not one of them is alone.**

❓<u>**Question of the day**</u>**: "**<u>**Isn't it neat that God even wants our teeth to have a twin so they aren't alone in our mouths?**</u>**"**

🧍 **"Does this candy necklace match my dress?"**

☂APRIL 21☂

🧍 **Mary Lu's response: "Who cares! It will only match or mismatch your dress for a few minutes!"**

✚ **To stay healthy, use the string to floss with after you devour the thing.**

📖 **2 Peter 3:3–6 First of all, you must understand that in the last days scoffers will come, scoffing and following their own evil desires. They will say, "Where is this 'coming' He promised? Ever since our fathers died, everything goes on as it has since the beginning of Creation." But they deliberately forget that long ago by God's Word the heavens existed and the Earth was formed out of water and by water. By these waters also the world of that time was deluged and destroyed.**

❓**Question of the day: "Are you a scoffer?"**

🕴 **"Seashells are usually found by the... sea. If you are lucky, you may be able to find some petrified shells in our cabin's backyard. That's right!"**

☂APRIL 22☂

🐱 **Witty Kitty's input: "When God flooded the entire Earth, everything got all stirred up and the valleys sunk down and the mountains arose and things like seashells and bones landed everywhere."**

✚ **Don't be a scoffer!**

📖 **John 14:27 Peace I leave with you; my peace I give you. I do not give to you as the world gives. Do not let your hearts be troubled and do not be afraid.**

?Question of the day: "Is there anything that is making your heart troubled today?"

👤 **"Learning to ride a tricycle is a big step! You are no longer a passenger in a stroller."**

☂APRIL 23☂

👤 **Baby No–No's relief: "Good, because I'm tired of being pushed around!"**

✚ **Give him about ten minutes.**

📖 **R**omans 13:10 Love does no harm to its neighbor. Therefore love is the fulfillment of the law.

❓**Question of the day: "Are we showing love to our neighbors?"**

👤 "If you are playing hopscotch in the country by the fence, which happens to be by the cow pasture, make sure you wear a pair of boots."

☂APRIL 24☂

🐕 Fudgy's tip: "And watch your step. Not only while playing hopscotch, but with everything you do in this life."

✚ Love your neighbor while you are at the fence.

📖 **Colossians 3:21 Fathers, do not embitter your children, or they will become discouraged.**

❓**Question of the day: "Are we building our children up or tearing them down?"**

🚶 **"It is pretty cute to watch a three–year–old playing soccer, but then again it's pretty cute to watch a three–year–old do just about anything."**

☔APRIL 25☔

🚶 **Baby No–No's experience: "It is pretty easy to entertain your grandparents who love you to pieces."**

✚ **Cherish every moment!**

📖 **Matthew 7:14 But small is the gate and narrow the road that leads to life, and only a few find it.**

❓**Question of the day: "Are you one of the few?"**

🧍 **"If you ask me for a straw while visiting us, just know that you will get one that has a few twists in it, just like the sliding board out back."**

☂APRIL 26☂

✏️ **Little Trooper's caution: "Just make sure you are on the straight and narrow path regarding your life."**

➕ **Keep both hands on the side rail and you'll be safe.**

📖 **P**roverbs 16:33 The lot is cast into the lap, but its every decision is from the Lord.

❓Question of the day: "When is the last time you rolled a Yahtzee?"

🧍 "It's raining at the cabin today, so Grandpa is getting out the Yahtzee game. The players who use the provided cup *sound* like they are having way more fun, however, the players who use their hands to roll the die actually are. They are much quicker. We will soon see who the winners are."

🌧APRIL 27🌧

🧍 Prince Roderick's comment: "I don't have a CHANCE!" (Definitely a cup user)

➕ Try to be a hands-on type parent and grandparent.

📖 **P**roverbs 12: 27 The lazy man does not roast his game, but the diligent man prizes his possessions.

❓Question of the day: "Do you prize things or use them as they are intended?"

🯅 "Trying a new food can be pretty scary, especially if you are a young child and someone you love is aiming a piece of broccoli or smashed peas at your face."

☂APRIL 28☂

🯅 Kimberella's experience: "That is nothing! Try to be an adult and have someone talk you into being brave enough to taste a chunk of octopus. Now *that's* scary!"

✚ Hunting and fishing are fine to participate in, but make sure you eat what you catch.

Psalm 113:3 From the rising of the sun to the place where it sets, the Name of the Lord is to be praised.

?Question of the day: "Do you praise the Lord each day?"

"I think the best cartoons are the ones that are played at the drive-in theater. It really doesn't make a difference which cartoon is showing. The feeling while watching them at the most beautiful time of day (dusk) can stay with you for a lifetime."

⚘APRIL 29⚘

Little Trooper's feeling: "I like the cartoon that has the dancing popsicles the best!"

✝ Thank you God for the beautiful sunrises and sunsets!

📖 **P**salm 78:23–25 Yet He gave a command to the skies above and opened the doors of the heavens; He rained down manna for the people to eat, He gave them the grain of Heaven. Men ate the bread of angels; He sent them all the food they could eat.

❓Question of the day: "Isn't this a great verse to remember in today's world?"

👤 "My father owns a grocery store and in it is something that begins with the letter... (fill in the blank.) This is a great game to play on long wagon rides to town."

☂APRIL 30☂

👤 Baby No–No's complaint: *"Until* we're all hungry and there isn't a grocery store for miles around!"

✚ "M" = "Manna"

📖 **Galatians 5:13 You, my brothers and sisters, were called to be free. But do not use your freedom to indulge the flesh; rather, serve one another humbly in love.**

❓**Question of the day: "Isn't freedom wonderful?"**

🧍 **"Freedom means being able to worship God in our churches, have a Bible study in our homes and choose where we want to live, which in our case is in a cabin in the sticks."**

❀MAY 1❀

🧍 **Mary Lu's question: "What does freedom mean to *you*?"**

✚ **Please don't ever take it for granted!**

📖 **Luke 6:31 Do to others as you would have them do to you.**

❓Question of the day: "Is the playing field on even ground?"

🚶 **"When it comes to playing four square on the playground called 'life', there are two kinds of people: those who try to keep the ball bouncing smoothly within the lines and those who will hit the ball as hard as possible to achieve as much pain as possible to their opponent. Which one are you?"**

❀MAY 2❀

🚶 **Lanore's answer: "Don't ask me...I'm a monkey bars type of kid."**

➕ **Please play nice!**

📖 **Acts 20:7** On the first day of the week we came together to break bread. Paul spoke to the people and, because he intended to leave the next day, kept on talking until midnight.

❓Question of the day: "Don't you think that Paul may have known that not much good happens after midnight?"

🚹 "Let's go on a picnic! We will need to pack a picnic basket, cooler, blanket and ant spray."

❀MAY 3❀

🐱 Witty Kitty's suggestion: "If it is going to be held on Grandma's and Grandpa's lawn behind the tool shed, you better consider adding snake repellant and ear plugs to your list."

✚ And a good pair of stomping boots.

🚹 (Eeeeew)

📖 **Isaiah 6:8 Then I heard the voice of the Lord saying, "Whom shall I send? And who will go for us?"**

❓Question of the day: "Are you willing to be sent where the Lord desires you to go?"

👤 **"If our grandchildren stay with us for a week at the cabin while their parents are out of town, they may be able to ride a school bus. It's out back all covered in weeds."**

❀MAY 4❀

👤 **Izzy Ann's hope: "Someday I would like to be able to paint that bus. Maybe Grandma and Grandpa will donate it to our church for field trips."**

✚ **It's nice to socialize!**

📖 **Ephesians 4:29** Do not let any unwholesome talk come out of your mouths, but only what is helpful for building others up according to their needs, that it may benefit those who listen.

❓Question of the day: "Are our words helpful or unwholesome?"

👤 "I think whoever invented the corndog is a genius! Too bad they haven't invented a corndog brat yet. Oh wait...they already did!"

❀MAY 5❀

🐕 Fudgy's rebuttal: "Not funny!"

✚ Please pass the mustard and don't get into name–calling.

📖 **M**ark 6:31 Then, because so many people were coming and going that they did not even have a chance to eat, He said to them, "Come with Me by yourselves to a quiet place and get some rest."

❓Question of the day: "Are you so busy coming and going some days that you don't have time to eat?"

🧍 "The perfect vacation for us involves relaxation, alone time, family time, good food, cool breezes or warm breezes and plenty of sleep. You know, it sounds a lot like a week here at our cabin."

✿MAY 6✿

🔖 Little Trooper's advice: "If you don't come apart (rest), then you will come apart."

➕ Nobody is too busy to rest once in a while.

📖 **P**roverbs 10:19 When words are many, sin is not absent, but he who holds his tongue is wise.

❓Question of the day: "Do you think this sounds simple?"

👤 "A good rule of thumb is to think before you start speaking. You cannot take back words once they are spoken. Too many words can be dangerous."

❀MAY 7❀

👤 Kimberella's motto: "If you don't say it, it can't be traced back to you."

✚ Zip it!

📖 **Proverbs 25:27** It is not good to eat too much honey, nor is it honorable to seek one's own honor.

❓**Question of the day: "Do you agree that it is better to be humble than to be proud?"**

👤 "Tummy aches are not fun. The best thing to do right away is to pray for God to make you feel better. The next thing to do is to eat some toast and slowly sip some white soda."

❀MAY 8❀

👤 Baby No–No's advice: "Don't eat a third dessert even if Grandma says it is okay to do so."

✚ Grandmas...gotta love 'em!

📖 **Ephesians 5:1–2 Be imitators of God, therefore, as dearly loved children and live a life of love, just as Christ loved us and gave Himself up for us as a fragrant offering and sacrifice to God.**

❓Question of the day: "Did you know that God can smell our offerings?"

🧍 **"When Grandpa says he wants a snack, I give him a choice of popcorn made over a fire, roasted marshmallows, homemade taffy, candied apple slices, maple fudge with nuts or gingerbread."**

❀MAY 9❀

🧍 **Lanore's observation: "How come all of Grandma's snacks also double as scents for candles?"**

✚ **Breathe deeply.**

📖 **Acts 1:14** They all joined together constantly in prayer, along with the women and Mary the mother of Jesus, and with His brothers.

❓**Question of the day: "When is the last time we have prayed constantly with others?"**

👤 **"Mother's Day is for all generations of moms. The best thing you can do for them is to wish them a 'Happy Mothers' Day!'"**

❀MAY 10❀

👤 **Izzy Ann's thought: "You can tell them you love them, too!"**

✝ **Thank you Mary, mother of Jesus!**

📖 **A**cts 22:16 And now what are you waiting for? Get up, be baptized and wash your sins away, calling on His Name.

❓Question of the day: "Well...?"

🧍 **"Grandpa's favorite color is white, that's why he likes to wear white shirts. He figures it's like a clean pallet for foods and drinks to spill on. I had the need to take a class in chemistry to remove stains just so he can start fresh the next morning."**

❀MAY 11❀

🐱 **Witty Kitty's wish: "Maybe someday he will miss his shirt and hit the floor for me to get a treat."**

✚ **Don't miss your chance to have your sins washed away by Jesus!**

📖 **1** Peter 5:3 ...not lording it over those entrusted to you, but being examples to the flock.

❓**Question of the day: "Are you being an example to someone in a good way?"**

👤 "Grandpa told me the other day that babysitting is a super way to earn a little extra money. Where else can you get paid to raid the refrigerator, play games and watch television?"

❁MAY 12❁

👤 Mary Lu's opinion: "Babysitting should be reserved for kids like me to do...not Grandma!"

✚ Try to always set a good example.

📖 **1** **Thessalonians 5:16–18 Be joyful always; pray continually; give thanks in all circumstances, for this is God's Will for you in Christ Jesus.**

❓**Question of the day: "How are we all doing on this one?"**

🧍 **"Today is Saturday, so we will head into town to the Farmers' Market to see what we can buy, sell or trade. How about two jars of honey for a bushel of apples?"**

🌸MAY 13🌸

🐕 **Fudgy's bargain: "How about skipping the apples and trading for two jars of caramel sauce?"**

✚ **How about being thankful for just plain apples.**

🐕 **(Sorry...)**

📖 **G**enesis 1:27 So God created man in His own image, In the image of God He created him; male and female He created them.

❓Question of the day: "Isn't it awesome to know that we are made in God's image?"

👤 "I think that whoever created flavored marshmallows is a genius. Now if we can get a few geniuses to change the lime flavored marshmallows, candies, gelatin, etc. to mint, a Nobel Peace Prize may be in order."

❁MAY 14❁

👤 Chew–Chew's desire: "Please just leave the marshmallows white and hand them over to me. Thanks!"

➕ No matter what color a marshmallow is, it is still a marshmallow. Same goes for humans – they are *all* mankind.

📖 **P**salm 4:8 There was a man all alone; he had neither son nor brother. There was no end to his toil, yet his eyes were not content with his wealth. "For whom am I toiling," he asked, "and why am I depriving myself of enjoyment?" This too is meaningless – a miserable business!

?Question of the day: "Do you wonder if this may have been a Monday or possibly every day?"

🚶 "There are so many reasons to go hiking around our cabin's property. You can do it for exercise, mudlarking, looking for antler sheds, snake skins, morels, berries, nuts and even arrowheads."

❀MAY 15❀

🚶 Izzy Ann's thought: "Or you can skip it and just keep sleeping in your cozy bed all morning long."

✝ You can look for bed bugs, mice, spiders...It works every time!

📖 **P**hilippians 2:14–16 Do everything without complaining or arguing, so that you may become blameless and pure, children of God without fault in a crooked and depraved generation, in which you shine like stars in the universe as you hold out the Word of Life – in order that I may boast on the day of Christ that I did not run or labor for nothing.

❓Question of the day: "Will you join me in trying not to complain or argue about things?"

🚹 "I remember back in the day eating a bowl of Alphabet Soup and never having the right shaped pasta to spell out any word completely."

❀MAY 16❀

🚹 Mary Lu's attempt: "V–I–O–L–I–N"

✚ N–O–T F–U–N–N–Y!

A-B-C

📖 **Proverbs 25:28 Like a city whose walls are broken down is a man who lacks self–control.**

❓**Question of the day: "Are your walls breaking?"**

🧍 **"I scream, they scream, the whole hay wagon screams when we see an ice cream stand in our travels to town."**

❀MAY 17❀

🐕 **Fudgy's warning: "If Grandpa hears screaming instead of 'please', he will keep on driving!"**

✚ **Please practice self–control.**

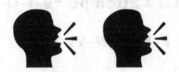

📖 **Ecclesiastes 3:13 That everyone may eat and drink and find satisfaction in all his toil – this is the gift of God.**

❓**Question of the day: "Do you enjoy your occupation?"**

👤 **"The definition found in the dictionary for the word 'kitchen' is: 'A room in which food is prepared'. It fails to mention it is also a place in which everyone seems to gather and crowd the cook as she is trying to fix their meal."**

🌸MAY 18🌸

🐱 **Witty Kitty's observation: "I notice that the cabin's kitchenette is used as a dropping off point for backpacks, shopping bags, library books and mail. It can also double as a dance floor."**

✝ **There are more things to complain about than this...so enjoy!**

📖 **P**salm 119:105 Your Word is a lamp to my feet and a light for my path.

?Question of the day: "Did you know that the Bible doesn't require batteries like a flashlight does?"

🧍 "The mail person out in the country stays in the truck that has the steering wheel on the other side of the vehicle so they can reach the mailbox on the road."

❀MAY 19❀

🧍 Chew–Chew's glee: "The Bible is God's love letter to us!"

✚ You may not be able to receive mail on Sundays, but the Bible is readable seven days a week!

📖 **Luke 19:1–4 Jesus entered Jericho and was passing through. A man was there by the name of Zacchaeus; he was a chief tax collector and was wealthy. He wanted to see who Jesus was, but being a short man he could not, because of the crowd. So he ran ahead and climbed a sycamore fig tree to see Him, since Jesus was coming that way.**

❓**Question of the day: "Don't you wish you were in the tree with him to see Jesus coming?"**

👤 **"If you want to climb a tree, please be careful! Choose one that has the main branches off of the trunk looking like a 'V' or a 'Y'.**

❀MAY 20❀

👤 **Lanore's warning: "Only climb as high as you care to fall...just in case."**

✚ **Please Lord let them not fall from any height!**

📖 **Genesis 32:12** "...But you have said, 'I will surely make you prosper and will make your descendants like the sand of the sea, which cannot be counted.'"

?Question of the day: "Have you ever tried to count just a handful of sand?"

🧍 "I don't mind if our grandchildren play in the sand box that is located behind the shed, but I *do* mind having sand in the kitchenette, sofa and bath tub."

❀MAY 21❀

🔖 Little Trooper's anguish: "I thought brooms were just for floors!"

✚ Don't sweep your sins under a rug, but instead, confess them to God.

📖 **M**atthew 18:10 "See that you do not look down on one of these little ones. For I tell you that their angels in Heaven always see the Face of My Father in Heaven."

❓Question of the day: "Doesn't this clear the subject up about every child having their own angel?"

👤 "I've noticed that babies really do not like baby swings until they are almost too big to squeeze their chubby legs into the holes. Ten year olds are the ones who are usually seen trying to stuff themselves into one."

❀MAY 22❀

👤 Baby No–No's observation: "When you are four years old, you're ready to move up to the bucket swing, but are too little yet and so you get swallowed up in the thing."

✚ Don't rush it kid...you're exactly the age you are supposed to be at this time.

📖 **Habakkuk 1:8** Their horses are swifter than leopards, fiercer than wolves at dusk. Their cavalry gallops headlong; their horsemen come from afar. They fly like a vulture swooping to devour;...

?Question of the day: "Do you have a new respect for horses?"

👤 **"Have you ever been on a covered bridge before? There is one down the road a piece that is made entirely of wood and sounds funny when tires roll over each plank."**

❀MAY 23❀

👤 **Prince Roderick's curiosity: "I wonder what it was like hearing horses' hooves clip-clopping on that bridge back in the day?"**

✚ **Wonderful!**

📖 **Luke 18:17** **"...I tell you the truth, anyone who will not receive the Kingdom of God like a little child will never enter it."**

?Question of the day: "Do you have faith like a little child?"

👤 **"I remember hearing a story about a famous scientist making a model of the Milky Way in his house and his atheist friend came over and asked him a few times who made it. The scientist kept replying that it just came about on its own. His friend just about lost his mind, because he *knew* that someone *had* to have made it, yet he just couldn't wrap his mind around the fact that God made the real Milky Way."**

❀MAY 24❀

👤 **Izzy Ann's belief: "God made everything on this Earth and all around it. Enough said."**

✚ **To enter into Heaven, we *must* have faith like a child...pure and simple!**

📖 **2** Timothy 2:3 Endure hardship with us like a good soldier of Christ Jesus.

❓<u>Question of the day: "Are we being good soldiers?"</u>

🚹 "Memorial Day is set aside to remember those who passed away whether this year or hundreds of years ago. Who do you remember on this day?"

❀MAY 25❀

🚹 Kimberella's response: "There are too many to remember them all, but I shall try!"

✝ God remembers everyone and everything!

📖 **P**salm 50:9-10 I have no need of a bull from your stall or of goats from your pens, for every animal of the forest is Mine, and the cattle on a thousand hills.

❓**Question of the day: "Any questions?"**

🧍 "I moo, you moo, we all moo to go to the zoo! At the cabin I am afraid the only animal you will see is a cow."

❀MAY 26❀

🐕 Fudgy's gripe: "What am I... chopped liver?!"

✚ What's your beef? Just realize you're lucky to be part of God's Creation!

📖 **P**salm 119:103 How sweet are Your Words to my taste, sweeter than honey to my mouth!

❓Question of the day: "<u>What else does one need?</u>"

👤 "I like pumpkin pie the best and my prince likes cherry. I can't stand peas and my husband can't stand sweet potatoes. We all have different taste buds and it is a good thing or else we would all be out of food to eat."

✿**MAY 27**✿

👤 Chew–Chew's question: "I wonder if we can get taste buds removed that have a negative attitude towards something that most people like?"

✚ No, because that is what makes up who you are.

📖 **R**omans 6:23 For the wages of sin is death, but the gift of God is Eternal Life in Christ Jesus our Lord.

❓Question of the day: "Did you accept God's free gift yet?"

👤 "Here is a scarf that I knitted for you. Nothing says 'love' like a homemade gift."

❀MAY 28❀

👤 Lanore's feeling: "Nothing says 'love' like sacrificing Your one and only Son so all of Your Creation can be forgiven!"

✝ Everyone on their own must accept His free gift to be saved!

📖 **P**roverbs 8:17 I love those who love Me, and those who seek Me find Me.

❓Question of the day: "Isn't this an awesome promise?"

👤 "We are out of marshmallows! Cut me a break! Speaking of breaks...why don't you all come spend a week of your summer with us at the cabin? It will promise to be great fun! (BYOM...Bring your own marshmallows.)"

✤MAY 29✤

👤 Mary Lu's hope: "Please let Grandma remember when she is buying more marshmallows to also pick up some of those almond cookies. They are a delicious substitute for graham crackers."

✚ You may want to pray about that, because right now she is searching high and low for her car keys.

📖 **1 Corinthians 6:11 And that is what some of you were. But you were washed, you were sanctified, you were justified in the Name of the Lord Jesus Christ and by the Spirit of our God.**

❓Question of the day: "Do you know Him?"

👤 "Sidewalk chalk is colorful, fun, entertaining and a creative tool for young children while playing outdoors."

❀MAY 30❀

👤 Izzy Ann's theory: "If you want your art to last and last, make sure to listen to the weather forecast beforehand. One rain storm could wash away a lot of work."

✝ Jesus can wash away your sins if you let Him – no matter how colorful a life you have lived!

📖 **Matthew 5:44–45 ...But I tell you: Love your enemies and pray for those who persecute you, that you may be sons of your Father in Heaven. He causes His sun to rise on the evil and the good, and sends rain on the righteous and the unrighteous.**

❓**Question of the day: "Do you love your enemies?"**

🚶 **"Staying at a cabin in the sticks can be home away from home for many of us. You just have to make sure not to stay the entire time inside the four walls so you can get plenty of fresh air and sunshine throughout the day. Then you will enjoy some of your best nights sleeping."**

🌸MAY 31🌸

🐈 **Witty Kitty's moment: "I like to nap up in the loft in front of that little window that overlooks the chicken coop. I get both sunshine and just enough breeze to...zzzzzzzzzz"**

✚ **Remember that God created the cat and knew exactly what He was doing.**

📖 **Genesis 1:21 So God created the great creatures of the sea and every living creature and moving thing with which the water teams, according to their kinds, and every winged bird according to its kind. And God saw that it was good.**

❓**Question of the day: "Do you know that this is where the swimming and land-dwelling dinosaurs come in?"**

🚶 **"Whenever I am at an ice cream stand, I try my best not to order a baby cone no matter how young the child is. For some reason they catch the word 'baby' being used and will have nothing to do with it."**

🚲 JUNE 1 🚲

🚶 **Baby No–No's scoop: "I personally like the chocolate dipped banana that is also referred to as a monkey tail."**

✚ **Monkeys have tails, but we do not – nor did we ever!**

📖 **James 3:8 "...but no man can tame the tongue. It is a restless evil, full of deadly poison."**

❓**Question of the day: "Is your tongue poisonous?"**

🧍 **"The only time it is okay to burst someone else's bubble is when they are getting too close to your face with bubble gum."**

🚲 JUNE 2 🚲

🧍 **Prince Roderick's tip: "The smaller the bubble, the louder the crack."**

✚ **Please watch your tongue and try not to stick it out!**

📖 **G**enesis 19:26 But Lot's wife looked back, and she became a pillar of salt.

❓<u>Question of the day</u>: <u>"Are we willing not to look back when we're told not to do so?"</u>

👤 "Grandpa thinks it is time to remove your training wheels and ride your bike the way it was designed to."

🚲 JUNE 3 🚲

👤 Chew–Chew's caution, "Whatever you do, don't look back!"

✚ Once your sins are forgiven, God doesn't rehash them. They are forgotten and so please do yourself a favor and move forward.

📖 **P**salm 3:5 I lie down and sleep; I wake again, because the Lord sustains me.

❗Question of the day: "Isn't it hard not to take getting up each morning for granted?"

🧍 **"Pillows can be a very personal item. If mine is too flat, I feel like I am on a sinking ship. If it is too puffy, I feel like I'm propped up on the side of an elephant's back. If it's just right, I could end up sleeping through breakfast. I just can't seem to win."**

🚲 JUNE 4 🚲

🐈 **Fudgy's suggestion: "Use your paws to rest your chin on like I do."**

➕ **The key to a great night's sleep is to work hard during the day and pray for a peaceful rest.**

🐈 **(Oh...)**

Revelation 10:10 I took the little scroll from the angel's hand and ate it. It tasted as sweet as honey in my mouth, but when I had eaten it, my stomach turned sour.

?Question of the day: "How many times have we eaten something a little too sweet?"

♛ "I bet there is a funny story behind the one who discovered popcorn. Grandpa is more interested in the story of the person who turned cow's milk into creamy butter. It just may be the same person."

🚲 JUNE 5 🚲

🐈 Witty Kitty's wish: "Someday I hope that the barn door gets left open so I can sneak in and drink some of that milk in the pail."

✝ God's Word is food for our souls!

📖 **P**salm 94:11 The Lord knows the thoughts of man; He knows that they are futile.

❓**Question of the day**: "**What are you thinking right now?**" (**God knows**)

🧍 "**Naughty words are just that... naughty. They are displeasing to your parents, grandparents, teachers, elders, etc. Most of all, they are displeasing to God.**"

🚲 **JUNE 6** 🚲

🔖 **Little Trooper's luck: I am not old enough to even talk yet, so no naughty words will come out of my mouth.**"

✚ **God knows every thought, so be careful!**

📖 **P**hilippians 4:9 Whatever you have learned or received or heard from me, or seen in me – put it into practice. And the God of Peace will be with you.

❓Question of the day: "Did you know that this is the way to have peace in your life?"

🧍 "Let's all go roller skating! I don't know who ever thought of putting wheels on the bottom of shoes, but they were a genius. Then again, the person who created the rubber stopper for the toe gets the safety award."

🚲 JUNE 7 🚲

🧍 Lanore's input: "While learning how to skate, one should do it at an indoor rink with skilled skaters and a medical team on the ready."

✚ Do not just skate through life. Take time to stop and smell the snack bar area!

📖 **G**enesis 1:29 Then God said, "I give every seed–bearing plant on the face of the whole Earth and every tree that has fruit with seed in it. They will be yours for food…"

❓<u>Question of the day</u>: "<u>Did you eat some seeds today along with your fruit?</u>"

🧍 "God made all kinds of fruit that comes in a variety of colors. Some of them you need to peel first like a banana, some you can choose to peel or not like an apple or you can just eat them 'as is' like a berry."

🚲 JUNE 8 🚲

🧍 Baby No–No's warning: "Don't peel a banana and especially don't cut one up for a four–year–old, otherwise the whole point of eating one is ruined."

✚ Remember to eat the seeds of each piece of fruit you are consuming. The Bible says to and it has been proven that seeds contain a small dose of cyanide that may prevent some types of cancer!

📖 **2 Corinthians 5:7 We live by faith, not by sight.**

❓**Question of the day: "Isn't it easy to see that we need faith more than anything?"**

👤 "I have sunglasses for my grandchildren in case it is an extremely sunny day and they forgot to bring them along. There are animals and geometric shapes and a rainbow of colors for them to choose from."

🚲 JUNE 9 🚲

👤 Izzy Ann's gripe: "Why is it that no matter what ones I pick out, they seem to have two smudges on the lenses that can't ever be removed?!"

✚ Don't let smudges alter your vision of what God has planned for your life!

📖 **P**salm 145:4 One generation will command your works to another; they will tell of your mighty acts.

❓<u>Question of the day: "What mighty acts have you performed lately?"</u>

🧍 "If you have great grandparents, consider yourself very lucky, because they know the most about your family history.... just ask them."

🚲 JUNE 10 🚲

🧍 Mary Lu's trivia question: "What has ears and can't hear?"

✚ Grandpa.

📖 **P**salm 141:3 Set a guard over my mouth, O Lord; keep watch over the door of my lips.

❓Question of the day: "Are our lips sealed or like an automatic garage door?"

👤 "Gum can come in all kinds of forms: flat sticks; barrel shapes; tubes; long ropes; large blocks; little squares, big and little balls. Would you like some?"

🚲 JUNE 11 🚲

🐈 Witty Kitty's complaint: "When you are done chewing the stuff, please don't throw it out in the yard!"

✚ To avoid a sticky situation, zip your lip and mind your own business. You'll be glad you did and so will the would–be listener.

📖 **M**atthew 7:6 "Do not give dogs what is sacred; do not throw your pearls to pigs. If you do, they may trample them under their feet, and then turn and tear you to pieces..."

❓Question of the day: "Don't you think that we should love our pets and not worship them?"

🚹 "If you go to the far corner of our property and look over the fence, you will be able to see some pigs on the neighbor's hobby farm. Why *did* that piggy go the market anyway?"

🚲 JUNE 12 🚲

🐈‍⬛ Fudgy's guess: "To buy Swiss cheese, rye bread, horseradish, BBQ sauce, lettuce and tomatoes?"

✚ You wish, Fudgy!

📖 **Matthew 13:30** "...Let both grow together until the harvest. At that time I will tell the harvesters: First collect the weeds and tie them in bundles to be burned; then gather the wheat and bring it into my barns.'"

❓**Question of the day: "Why do weeds grow so quickly and plentifully?"**

👤 "Weeds are those useless plants that grow like...well... like weeds! Even though they get sprayed, stomped on by a herd of cattle, starved and even burned. They usually choke out the flowers, vegetables and crops that are well-taken care of."

🚲 JUNE 13 🚲

👤 Baby No–No's questions: "Why?"

✝ For us to understand the parables in the Bible, that's why.

👤 (Oh...)

📖 **M**atthew 15:11 "...What goes into a man's mouth does not make him 'unclean', but what comes out of his mouth, that is what makes him 'unclean.'"

❓<u>Question of the day</u>: "<u>Should we go brush our teeth again and take another swig of mouthwash?</u>"

🧍 "I tend to remind Grandpa to sit up straight, stand erect, hold his head up, keep his chin up, not to slump and throw his shoulders back. With proper posture, your internal organs will be able to function more effectively."

🚲 JUNE 14 🚲

🧍 Chew–Chew's reality: "I'm always told not to talk with my mouth full. Does *that* help anything?"

✚ Yes...it keeps your parents happy.

🧍 (Oh...)

📖 **P**roverbs 27:17 As iron sharpens iron, so one man sharpens another.

❓Question of the day: "How sharp are you and your fellow man?"

🧍 "I think that a computer can be a very useful tool when used properly. The problem is, we don't have internet out here in the sticks."

🚲 JUNE 15 🚲

🧍 Lanore's anguish: "There goes MY FACE!!"

✚ Socializing is great for your health. God created us to be around others!

Proverbs 17:17 A friend loves at all times, and a brother is born for adversity.

?Question of the day: "Do you love at all times...even those who are hard to love?"

"In the city, I suppose that skateboarding is a quick way to get around. Out here in the country, you are better off in a wheelbarrow powered by your big brother."

⚲ JUNE 16 ⚲

Little Trooper's concern: "Am I the brother that is supposed to get the ride or do the powering?"

✚ Relax...nothing is expected out of you yet, except to be cute at all times.

📖 **L**uke 14:28 "Suppose one of you wants to build a tower. Will he not first sit down and estimate the cost to see if he has enough money to complete it?..."

❓**Question of the day: "How many financial problems would be solved if the world followed this advice?"**

👤 "Water towers in our part of Iowa look like rocket ships ready to be shot off into space."

🚲 JUNE 17 🚲

👤 Izzy Ann's dream: "I hope they always look that–away!"

✚ Looks will come and go, but what's in your heart is what really matters.

📖 **P**salm 72:6 He will be like rain falling on a mown field, like showers watering the earth.

❓**Question of the day: "Don't you think that this means that it would be a lovely feeling?"**

👤 "Grandpa just told me it is a good day for ducks. That means it's raining like crazy and there should be plenty of puddles for our grandchildren to jump in."

🚲 JUNE 18 🚲

👤 Kimberella's reminder: "Don't forget your raincoats!"

✚ God must have used his paint brush when He created the male mallard duck.

📖 **Matthew 25:30 ...And throw that worthless servant outside, into the darkness, where there will be weeping and gnashing of teeth.'...**

❓**Question of the day: "Wouldn't that be a horrible place to be?"**

🧍 "My grandkids brought along their allowances just in case we take a trip into town. Let's go!"

🚲 JUNE 19 🚲

🧍 Chew–Chew's prediction: "I bet Grandma will forget *her* allowance and ask to borrow a dime from each of us for her salt water taffy fix...and some dental floss."

✝ God gave you teeth, so please try your best to take care of them.

📖 **M**ark 6:31 Then, because so many people were coming and going that they did not even have a chance to eat, He said to them, "Come with Me by yourselves to a quiet place and get some rest."

❓**Question of the day: "Where is your quiet place?"**

🚶 "Summer can be hot, steamy and unpleasant, but...it can also be the best season of the year for fun!"

🚲 **JUNE 20** 🚲

🚶 Mary Lu's comment: "There isn't any school in June, so we get to go to the beach on the river, play outside, go camping and travel!"

✝ Do not forget church picnics, family reunions and time spent with the old folks at the cabin!

📖 **P**roverbs 23:22 Listen to your father, who gave you life, and do not despise your mother when she is old.

❓<u>Question of the day</u>: "<u>Do we always respect our parents?</u>"

👤 "Fathers' Day is celebrated by new daddies, middle–aged dads and old and very old grandfathers."

🚲 JUNE 21 🚲

✏️ Little Trooper's blessing: "May all daddies out there have a Happy Fathers' Day... you all deserve it!"

✝️ Don't forget to give thanks to our God Father Almighty!

📖 **P**salm 104:5 He set the Earth on its foundations; it can never be moved.

❓**Question of the day: "Did I just read the word 'NEVER'?" (Yes, I did)**

🧍 "Look at Izzy Ann go 'round and 'round on the merry–go–round! Oh wait...Izzy Ann looks dizzy and not so merry anymore!"

🚲 **JUNE 22** 🚲

🧍 Izzy Ann's conclusion: "I think I'll just stick with the see–saw."

✚ It is far better if you don't go around in circles all of your life, but practice living a balanced life.

📖 **R**oman 12:2 "...Do not conform any longer to the pattern of this world, but be transformed by the renewing of your mind. Then you will be able to test and approve what God's Will is – His good, pleasing and perfect Will."

❓Question of the day: "Do you know what God's Will is for you?"

🚶 "Having a positive attitude can be very good for your health, both physically and mentally. It will also be helpful at the cabin to keep up the joyfulness."

🚲 JUNE 23 🚲

🚶 Lanore's belief: "Nobody likes doom and gloom."

✚ The only dark cloud over your head should be sky–high!

📖 **Proverbs 29:11 A fool gives full vent to his anger, but a wise man keeps himself under control.**

❓Question of the day: "Do we appear to others as a fool or a wise man?"

🧍 **"Today we are going to take Mary Lu, Izzy Ann, Lanore, Chew–Chew, Baby No–No and Little Trooper to the country version of a theme park that just opened last week. It is about thirty minutes from here."**

🚲 JUNE 24 🚲

🧍 **Chew–Chew's report: "Just getting there was like riding a rollercoaster. Grandpa drove on a road that had lots of ups and downs and hairpin turns. Grandma sure can scream!"**

✚ **A physical rollercoaster is much better than an emotional one.**

📖 **Proverbs 27:3 Stone is heavy and sand a burden, but provocation by a fool is heavier than both.**

❓**Question of the day: "Why drag around that extra ball and chain?"**

🚶 **"There is a beach in the country called Sandy Land. It is located on the river and it's the best place to be *until* you wade in the water and the sand turns to mud.**

🚲 JUNE 25 🚲

🐱 **Witty Kitty's thought: "Eeeew!"**

✝ **Since God created us out of dirt and we are mostly made of water, then why aren't we a big blob of mud? Because God is in control.**

🚶 **(Oh...)**

📖 **John 21:6 He said, "Throw your net on the right side of the boat and you will find some." When they did, they were unable to haul the net in because of the large number of fish.**

❓**Question of the day: "Are you on the right side of life?"**

🚶 **"If you go fishing on the pond in the back corner of our property, you may catch more than just fish."**

🚲 JUNE 26 🚲

🚶 **Prince Roderick's advice: "Unless you *like* the taste of cooked tires, sticks, lily pads and snakes, I would suggest you fish in the 'Big Drink' instead."**

✚ **You are supposed to fish out of the right side of the boat.**

📖 John 8:7 When they kept on questioning Him, He straightened up and said to them, "If any one of you is without sin, let him be the first to throw a stone at her."

❓**Question of the day: "Do you hear all those stones dropping?"**

🚹 "I bet God gave you a talent that you can use to make a homemade gift for a loved one. Even if it is singing them a song with your voice!"

🚲 JUNE 27 🚲

🚹 Izzy Ann's talent: "I can throw a rock from here to the moon."

✚ Please pray that she doesn't draw Grandpa's name this year!

📖 **D**euteronomy 22:6–7 If you come across a bird's nest beside the road, either in a tree or on the ground, and the mother sitting on the young or on the eggs, do not take the mother with the young. You may take the young, but be sure to let the mother go, so that it may go well with you and you may have a long life.

❓Question of the day: "Got it?"

👤 "Out in the sticks, you can find plenty of wood to start a camp fire or even build a house with them."

🚲 JUNE 28 🚲

🐕 Fudgy's two cents: "Now *that* would make a big dog house for me!"

✚ You know what they say about 'sticks and stones'...and the 'Word' can only help you.

Luke 2:10 But the angel said to them, "Do not be afraid. I bring you good news of great joy that will be for all the people..."

?Question of the day: "What is there to be afraid of when we know that Jesus Christ died on the cross for all of our sins so we can spend Eternity with Him no matter what happens to us here on Earth...even death of our bodies?"

"When we read the Bible at night in our cabin, we especially like the books of Matthew, Mark, Luke and John. They are called "Good News".

⚘ JUNE 29 ⚘

Kimberella's info: "There is a good reason that they are referred to as such!"

✚ Did you read *your* Bible today?

📖 **P**hilippians 4:9 Whatever you have learned or received or heard from Me, or seen in Me – put it into practice. And the God of Peace will be with you.

?Question of the day: "Maybe we should say that practice makes peace instead of perfect?"

🧍 "Let's play 'Bible Challenge'. It is a fun trivia game of who, why, what, where and when. The more you play it, the more you soak in."

🚲 JUNE 30 🚲

🧍 Mary Lu's thoughts: "It can even make a kid feel like a Bible scholar. In fact, they have a children's version, which Grandma and Grandpa like to play with me."

✚ It really works!

📖 **1 Corinthians 14:40 But everything should be done in a fitting and orderly way.**

❓**Question of the day: "How are your organizational skills lately?"**

👤 **"I'm sure that having a piggy bank at your grandparents' cabin is kind of strange, but what is even stranger is having saved up coins at our cabin with nowhere to spend them."**

🏴JULY 1🏴

👤 **Chew–Chew's confusion: "How come it's more fun to do chores at Grandma and Grandpa Buckskins' cabin and get paid for them than at my own house?"**

➕ **Probably because you don't live there among the mess. It is a different kind of cleaning up.**

👤 **(This is true...)**

📖 **Luke 10:19 I have given you authority to trample on snakes and scorpions and to overcome all the power of the enemy; nothing will harm you.**

❓**Question of the day: "Do you want to go first?"**

🧍 **"The only time I don't mind seeing a snake is on the 4th of July when Grandpa is entertaining the grandchildren with those black looking fireworks."**

🎏JULY 2🎏

🐱 **Witty Kitty's headache: "I can't stand the level of screaming that Grandma can produce whenever she sees a real snake out back. It's *almost* as loud as when she sees a bat."**

➕ **Snakes help keep the mice away, but then again...so do mouse traps.**

📖 **1** Samuel 16:7 But the Lord said to Samuel, "Do not consider his appearance or his height, for I have rejected him. The Lord does not look at the things man looks at. Man looks at the outward appearance, but the Lord looks at the heart."

❓Question of the day: "Wouldn't it be a better world if all of us looked at the heart of each person we meet?"

🧍 "Babies sure are cute! It just proves that God appreciates 'cute'. I wonder if He sees all of us that way even when we become very old."

⚐JULY 3⚐

✏️ Little Trooper's question: "Does God think we are cute even when we're naughty?"

✚ Probably not, Baby.

📖 Isaiah 43:2 "...When you pass through the waters, I will be with you; and when you pass through the rivers, they will not sweep over you. When you walk through the fire, you will not be burned; the flames will not set you ablaze."

❓Question of the day: "Who else do you need in times of trouble?"

👤 "Today is Independence Day. Look out! Grandpa likes to hand out sparklers, set fire to snakes, shoot off caps and scare me with bottle rockets flying off the front porch."

🏴JULY 4🏴

👤 Baby No-No's fear: "I just hope they don't forget about me when they are running all over the place."

✚ Jesus will calm your fears and never leave you. Why not ask Him into your life?

📖 **Hebrews 10:25** Let us not give up meeting together, as some are in the habit of doing, but let us encourage one another – and all the more as you see the Day approaching.

❓<u>Question of the day: "Doesn't it sound like we are supposed to socialize with other Christians?"</u>

👤 "Let's all load up in the hay wagon and head to the Open Door–See People Church. Kids, you can go to Sunday school and learn about the Father, Son and Holy Spirit. Grandpa and I will go to the church service and do the same."

🏳️JULY 5🏳️

👤 Izzy Ann's glee: "I just remembered... there is a picnic today!"

✚ You just can't beat socializing with other people who have the same faith as you do!

📖 **1 Chronicles 16:36 Praise be to the Lord, the God of Israel, from Everlasting to Everlasting. Then all the people said "Amen" and "Praise the Lord."**

?Question of the day: "Can I get an 'Amen'?"

🧍 **"Remember that you can pray at any time of the day or night and directly to God in Jesus' Name."**

🎏**JULY 6**🎏

🧍 **Lanore's reminder: "Use the words 'please' and 'thank you' while doing so."**

✚ **And use the word 'Amen', which means: 'I believe'.**

📖 **J**ames 1:5 If any of you lacks wisdom, he should ask God, who gives generously to all without finding fault, and it will be given to him.

❓**Question of the day: "Have you asked for wisdom this morning?"**

🕴 **"Time out isn't any fun for the naughty child or the person who ordered it. Whatever you do, don't let yourself, whether young _or_ old, get into a permanent 'time out' with God."**

㋡**JULY 7**㋡

🐈 **Fudgy's worry: "What if you're in time out more than you are part of the group?"**

✚ **Do more thinking while sitting in the corner... and better yet, pray for wisdom.**

📖 **N**ehemiah 9:11 You divided the sea before them, so that they passed through it on dry ground, but You hurled their pursuers into the depths, like a stone into mighty waters.

?Question of the day: "Are you in deep waters?"

👤 "Most of us know that Moses crossed the Red Sea along with lots of other people, but did you know that there are other times mentioned in the Bible of other bodies of water either being parted, bunched up or dried up?"

♪JULY 8♪

👤 Prince Roderick's addition: "I like to watch documentaries on evidence of the Red Sea Crossing."

✚ Other verses: Exodus 14:21–22; Joshua 3:15–17; 2 Kings 2:7–8 & 13–14

📖 **Genesis 11:4 Then they said, "Come, let us build ourselves a city, with a tower that reaches to the heavens, so that we may make a name for ourselves and not be scattered over the face of the whole Earth."**

❓**Question of the day: "Don't you think that sometimes we try to make a name for ourselves rather than give God all the Glory?"**

👤 **"When Grandpa was a little boy, he liked it very much to be able to play with building blocks. If you are strong enough, you might be able to pry his fingers off of them so you can create something."**

🏁JULY 9🏁

🐱 **Witty Kitty's deal: "I stay high up on a shelf above the fireplace to keep from getting hit on the head by a falling stack of blocks!"**

✚ **We must have it in us to try to build things as high as we can get away with – like the tower of Babel, for example.**

📖 **R**evelation 22:2 ...down the middle of the great street of the city. On each side of the river stood the Tree of Life, bearing twelve crops of fruit, yielding its fruit every month. And the leaves of the tree are for the healing of the nations.

❓Question of the day: "Wouldn't it be nice if we could use that tree now for the healing of the nations?"

👤 "God made vegetables in a variety of colors and shapes. Some I need to cook (Brussel sprouts), some I choose to cook or not (carrots) and some I don't even think about cooking (lettuce.) Except for that one time...yuck!"

🏴JULY 10🏴

✏️ Little Trooper's comment: "Welcome to my world."

✝️ God knew what He was doing when He made vegetables and fruits in different colors. They are both pleasing to the eye and each color has its own health benefits.

📖 **D**aniel 1:16 So the guard took away their choice food and the wine they were to drink and gave them vegetables instead.

❓**Question of the day: "Did you know that they ended up being stronger by making the switch?"**

👤 **"Speaking of vegetables...If you don't care for the pajamas with feet in them that I gave you for Christmas last year, then eat a second or third helping of veggies each day and you will eventually grow out of them."**

🏳️JULY 11🏳️

👤 **Chew–Chew's prediction: "Then we'll probably end up getting a bigger size for Christmas this year!"**

✚ **Never get too big for your britches!**

📖 **G**enesis 9:1 Then God blessed Noah and his sons, saying to them, "Be fruitful and increase in number and fill the Earth..."

?Question of the day: "What could possibly be better than having God's blessing?"

🧍 "The grandkiddies like to see us 'kid' around with our siblings and try to picture each of us in our childhood homes growing up with them together."

🎏JULY 12🎏

🧍 Mary Lu's realization: "It is weird to think that each one of Grandma's siblings and herself were inside of Great Grandma's tummy."

✚ It's not weird...it's life.

📖 **Proverbs 29:20 Do you see a man who speaks in haste? There is more hope for a fool than for him.**

❓**Question of the day: "Do you know that haste usually makes waste?"**

👤 **"Swimming pools are really just enormous bathtubs. The only difference is the thirty foot sliding board at one end. Let's go to town and cool off!"**

🏁JULY 13🏁

👤 **Izzy Ann's hope: "*Please* let there be plenty of ice cream and popcorn at the concession stand!"**

✚ **Just like waiting to swim after eating, you should wait to speak *after* thinking.**

📖 **Jeremiah 31:29–30 "In those days people will no longer say, 'The fathers have eaten sour grapes, and the children's teeth are set on edge.' Instead, everyone will die for his own sin; whoever eats sour grapes – his own teeth will be set on edge..."**

❓Question of the day: "Do you have sour grapes in your life?"

👤 **"I think what is stranger than losing baby teeth, is *not* losing them. Actually, it's not *that* strange, because quite a few folks have one or more of them still in their mouths even as adults well into their years."**

🏳JULY 14🏳

👤 **Lanore's explanation: "It's because they never had an adult tooth to push the baby tooth out."**

✚ **Okay, it *is* strange –there, I said it!**

📖 John 3:16 "For God so loved the world that He gave His one and only Son, that whoever believes in Him shall not perish but have Eternal Life..."

❓Question of the day: "Did you receive God's perfect gift that is His Son, Jesus Christ?"

👤 "What is the difference between suntan lotion and sun screen anyway?"

⚑JULY 15⚑

💊 Little Trooper's answer: "A couple of generations."

➕ You can get too much 'sun', but never too much 'Son'!

📖 **J**ohn 15:13 Greater love has no one than this: that He lay down His life for His friends.

❓**Question of the day: "Who else would lay his life down for all of us sinners?"**

🧍 **"Beach towels can be as personal as your very own bicycle. Grandpa has Scooby Doo and mine is Strawberry Shortcake. What does your towel say about you?"**

🏴**JULY 16**🏴

🐈 **Fudgy's admission: "Mine is BRATZ."**

➕ Choose your towel and your friends very carefully!

📖 **P**roverbs 28:25 A greedy man stirs up dissension, but he who trusts in the Lord will prosper.

❓**Question of the day: "Would you rather be greedy or prosper by trusting God?"**

🕴 "Bubble gum, bubble gum in a dish. How many pieces do you wish?"

⚐**JULY 17**⚐

🕴 Lanore's reply: "All of them!"

✚ Please don't be greedy!

? ● ● ● ?

📖 **P**roverbs 25:27 It is not good to eat too much honey, nor is it honorable to seek one's own honor.

❓<u>Question of the day: "Did you know that you could eat too much honey?"</u>

👤 "Shall we talk about cotton candy? Maybe we should just eat it instead and talk later."

🏳️ JULY 18 🏳️

👤 Izzy Ann's concern: "Don't we speak more clearly when our teeth are still intact?"

✝️ Moderation is the key.

📖 **1 John 4:8 Whoever does not love does not know God, because God is love.**

❓**Question of the day: "Do you have love in your heart?"**

🧍 **"O = Hugs; ♥ = Love – In my world they both mean love and peace."**

⚑JULY 19⚑

✏️ **Little Trooper's reality: "They mean that to me, too!"**

✚ **Tell someone you love them today!**

📖 **Job 9:27–28 If I say, 'I will forget my complaint, I will change my expression, and smile', I still dread all my sufferings, for I know you will not hold me innocent.**

❓**Question of the day: "What are you suffering from today?"**

🧍 **"Body language can say a lot about us. If you have your arms folded, you may appear to be mad. If you rest your head on your fist, you may look bored. If you see me half–way falling off of the couch, I may *look* tired, but I'm really just searching for my glasses."**

🎏**JULY 20**🎏

🐕 **Fudgy's body language: "If you see me showing my teeth, I'm not going to bite you. It's probably a case of peanut butter sticking to the roof of my mouth."**

✚ **If you seem to have negative looking body language, but don't mean anything by it, just remember to smile and people who see you won't be offended.**

📖 **1** Timothy 5:8 If anyone does not provide for his relatives, and especially for his immediate family, he has denied the faith and is worse than an unbeliever.

?Question of the day: "How have we been treating our relatives recently?"

🚶 "Why go to the circus when we have a jungle gym out back, animals of all kinds that can perform tricks, bicycles that have multiple wheels, shelled peanuts and Grandma's kitchenette for treats?"

🏁JULY 21🏁

🐱 Witty Kitty's answer: "To see our kinfolk, that's why!"

✚ No matter how 'different' your relatives may be, please go visit them from time–to–time.

📖 **Proverbs 31:21 When it snows, she has no fear for her household; for all of them are clothed in scarlet.**

❓Question of the day: "Are you ready for winter that you know is coming?"

🧍 **"Grandpa doesn't have a garage on his property, but he *does* have a couple of sheds, a small barn and a snow cone stand."**

⚐**JULY 22**⚐

🧍 **Baby No–No's correction: "Make that Grandma's snow cone stand."**

✚ **Oh yeah!**

📖 **John 6:35 Then Jesus declared, "I am the Bread of Life. He who comes to Me will never go hungry, and he who believes in Me will never be thirsty.**

❓**Question of the day: "Isn't this truth wonderful?"**

👤 **"I do not think there are too many things better than the county fair. Hay wagons, animals, more snacks than you can shake a stick at, chain saw carving, demolition derby, music, rides for the kiddies and art displays."**

🏳️ JULY 23 🏳️

👤 **Chew–Chew's question: "Isn't that what we already have at Grandma's and Grandpa's cabin?"**

✚ **Life *is* serious, but mixing in some innocent fun doesn't hurt now and then.**

📖 **Proverbs 22:29** Do you see a man skilled in his work? He will serve before kings; he will not serve before obscure men.

❓**Question of the day: "What are your skills?"**

🧍 **"Our art projects for this year include":**
- **Mary Lu – Frog**
- **Izzy Ann –Butterfly**
- **Lanore – Cat**
- **Chew–Chew –Dinosaur**
- **Baby No–No – Duck**
- **Little Trooper – Puppy**
- **Grandma Buckskin – Mannequin 'dressed' in an outfit made of yarn**

ꄆ**JULY 24**ꄆ

🧍 **Prince Roderick's curiosity: "Why?!"**

✝ **Because God gave them the talent to create, that's why.**

🧍 **(Oh...)**

📖 **Genesis 9:3 Everything that lives and moves will be food for you. Just as I gave you the green plants, I now give you everything.**

❓**Question of the day: "Do you realize that before the flood man and animals didn't eat meat?"**

👤 "Our grandchildren *were* going to raise rabbits to show at this year's fair, but Fudgy and Witty Kitty had other plans…"

🏳JULY 25🏳

👤 Kimberella's disgust: "I've heard of pets eating kids' homework, but *this* is ridiculous!"

✝ After the flood of Noah's day, God let animals and humans chase and eat animals for food.

📖 **Proverbs 13:3 He who guards his lips guards his life, but he who speaks rashly will come to ruin.**

❓Question of the day: "This advice sounds serious, don't you think?"

🧍 **"You should *always* be polite even if the other person is not. You don't have to go on a picnic with them, just mind your manners and keep silent *unless* you have something nice to say to them."**

🏴JULY 26🏴

🧍 **Baby No–No's frustration: "I have plenty of nice things to say, but nobody seems to be able to understand me at this stage of life."**

✚ **Just keep trying.**

📖 **1 Corinthians 3:16 Don't you know that you yourselves are God's temple and that God's Spirit lives in you?**

❓**Question of the day: "How are you taking care of God's temple?"**

👤 "Every town, no matter how small it is, seems to have some sort of a landmark. It can be an old building ready to fall down, statue, fountain, large sign, water tower or even a strawberry that weighs over a ton."

🏳JULY 27🏳

👤 Mary Lu's joy: "I like the little village that has an ice cream cone as tall as a giraffe!"

✚ There are many landmarks mentioned in the Bible that are still visible today.

📖 **A**cts 27:35 After He said this, He took some bread and gave thanks to God in front of them all. Then He broke it and began to eat.

❓Question of the day: "Do you give thanks to God before your meals?"

🧍 "Grandpa is firing up the grill. I wonder if he is going to cook hamburgers, steaks or hot dogs."

🏁**JULY 28**🏁

🧍 Chew–Chew's conclusion: "None of the above. He is cooking frog legs and duck."

✚ After you give thanks for your meal, make sure you have plenty of ketchup to pass around and a few anti–acid tablets.

📖 **E**xodus 20:12 "Honor your father and your mother, so that you may live long in the land the Lord your God is giving you..."

❓**Question of the day: "Doesn't this give you a new respect for the Commandment to honor your father and mother?"**

🧍 "Do you happen to have a brother or sister who looks like you? Don't worry...in about fifty years you will all look like your parents *or* your aunts and uncles."

🏳️JULY 29🏳️

🧍 Izzy Ann's trauma: "But we already *do* look like our parents!"

✚ Get over it kid and consider yourself lucky.

📖 **Matthew 26:41** "Watch and pray so that you will not fall into temptation. The spirit is willing, but the body is weak."

❓Question of the day: "Did you know that praying is more important than taking your vitamins every day?"

👤 "I have a candy dish in every room of our cabin. Luckily for the children, there are a lot of rooms in here."

🎏 **JULY 30** 🎏

👤 Lanore's addition: "Luckily for Grandma, she counts the front porch, back deck and carport as rooms."

✚ **Don't give into temptation!**

📖 **Isaiah 41:10 So do not fear, for I am with you; do not be dismayed, for I am your God. I will strengthen you and help you; I will uphold you with My righteous Right Hand.**

❓<u>Question of the day: "How can we be fearful when we're held in God's Hand?"</u>

🧍 **"When you are situated in the country, it can be pretty scary when the sun goes down, because it gets very dark with the absence of bright city lights."**

🏴JULY 31🏴

🐕 **Fudgy's idea: "I can use my nose to guide me to my food dish and the garbage can."**

➕ **Be afraid of no one or nothing, just have a fear of God, because He is Almighty!**

📖 **G**enesis 7:11 In the six hundredth year of Noah's life, on the seventeenth day of the second month – on that day all the springs of the great deep burst forth, and the flood gates of the heavens were opened.

?Question of the day: "Do you think that maybe the reason God decided to tell us the precise date is so the reader believes that it really happened?"

🧍 "The grandchildren have been bugging me for weeks to go to a splash pad so they can have water shoot up at them on a sweltering day. We never had those things when we were kids."

○AUGUST 1○

🧍 Prince Roderick's memory: "I liked to shoot at my siblings with those little water guns. Now they make them as big as a cannon!"

✚ If you want to see how God can shoot up water, go to Yellowstone Park in Wyoming and see the Old Faithful Geyser.

📖 **2 Corinthians 9:7 Each man should give what he has decided in his heart to give, not reluctantly or under compulsion, for God loves a cheerful giver.**

❓Question of the day: "What does your heart say you should give?"

🚹 **"A savings account at your local bank is a safe place to keep your money for future use. Remember to give some of it back to God, since He is the one who helped you earn it."**

⚬AUGUST 2⚬

🍼 **Little Trooper's hope: "Someday I would like to have a piggy bank that has a huge appetite."**

✚ **Have you thought about a way that you can give back to God with your time, talent and/or treasure?**

📖 **L**uke 12:22–23 Then Jesus said to His disciples: "Therefore I tell you, do not worry about your life, what you will eat; or about your body, what you will wear. Life is more than food, and the body more than clothes…"

?Question of the day: "Do you worry about nothing and prayer about everything?"

🧍 "Slippers are so warm and cozy to wear on the frosty floor boards in our cabin. Since it is August right now, I would like to experience a touch of frostiness on the bottom of my feet."

○AUGUST 3○

🐈 **Witty Kitty's gripe:** "How come Fudgy gets to wear cute doggy shoes and a sweater when it's cold out and I don't?"

✚ Because you are a cat and cats don't like to get dressed up.

🐈 (Oh…)

📖 **P**hilippians 4:13 I can do everything through Him who gives me strength.

❓**Question of the day: "Are you ready to dive in?"**

🧍 "Did you ever notice that when you hurt just one finger or thumb, you all of a sudden realize how much you use that particular digit all day long?"

☼ AUGUST 4 ☼

🧍 Kimberella's frustration: "Opening a pickled beet jar is the worst!"

✚ Don't take things for granted – especially pickled beets.

📖 **John 14:26 But the Counselor, the Holy Spirit, whom the Father will send in My Name, will teach you all things and will remind you of everything I have said to you.**

❓Question of the day: "Isn't this marvelous?"

🚶 **"The Holy Spirit (a.k.a. the Holy Ghost) guides me throughout my day. Do *you* have the Holy Spirit dwelling inside of *you*?"**

○AUGUST 5○

🚶 **Baby No–No's hint: "All you have to do is ask Jesus Christ to forgive your sins and ask Him to come into your life and the Holy Spirit will dwell inside of you."**

✝ **And then try your hardest to live the rest of your life for Him!**

📖 **E**cclesiastes 12:12 Be warned, my son, of anything in addition to them. Of making many books there is no end, and much study wearies the body.

?Question of the day: "Are you weary?"

🜂 "I hope my grandchildren will remember to bring their library books with them this weekend. I enjoy reading to them and especially like listening to *them* reading the stories to *me*."

⚬AUGUST 6⚬

🜂 Izzy Ann's delight: "It is so much fun watching Grandma's eyes grow big as I read her a pop-up book!"

✝ They sell pop-up Bible stories as well.

📖 Jonah 1:17 But the Lord provided a great fish to swallow Jonah, and Jonah was inside the fish three days and three nights.

❓Question of the day: "Wouldn't it have been a lot easier for Jonah to obey God?"

🧍 "Jonah was swallowed by a huge fish and was inside of it for three days. Since He didn't obey God and tried to do something else rather than take His advice, he made a nice temporary snack."

○ AUGUST 7 ○

🧍 Prince Roderick's rest of the story: "Then Jonah was thrown up out of the fish onto dry ground."

✚ Don't get swallowed up in the ways of the world. Follow God's advice with a cheerful attitude!

📖 **G**enesis 1:27 "...So God created man in His own image, in the image of God He created him; male and female He created them."

❓**Question of the day: "Did you count three times in this one sentence that God created humans?"**

🧍 "I think it is important to learn how to comb your hair every morning so you don't look like you just rolled out of bed in the middle of the day."

◦AUGUST 8◦

🐕 Fudgy's critique: "Grandma Buckskin's hair always looks like it has party going on."

✚ No matter if you are bald, or have a ton of hair that does its own thing, please remember that God designed *you* to be *you* from your feet all the way up to the top of your head!

📖 **1 Thessalonians 5:16–18 Be joyful always; pray continually; give thanks in all circumstances, for this is God's Will for you in Christ Jesus.**

?Question of the day: "What are you thankful for today?"

🧍 **"Swimsuits are so comfortable to wear when you are a child, whether they are playing in a pool or just running around the yard on a very hot afternoon. Enjoy!"**

○AUGUST 9○

🧍 **Mary Lu's joy: "I like it when Grandpa fills up the big metal wash tub for us to sit in while we eat our Popsicles!"**

✚ **Remember to say 'thank you' for even the little things your grandparents do for you.**

📖 **2** Timothy 1:5 I have been reminded of your sincere faith, which first lived in your grandmother Lois and in your mother Eunice and, I am persuaded, now lives in you also.

❓Question of the day: "Are you going to pass your faith onto your descendants?"

👤 "Jacks can be a fun game to play on a shaded back porch or on your bedroom's floor. You may need to ask a great grandparent for instructions to play, however, since they are experts on the subject."

○AUGUST 10○

👤 Lanore's question: "Can a great grandparent sit cross–legged on the floor for more than a minute?!"

✚ Call them up and ask them onesie or twosie questions and found out foursie yourself!

📖 **1** Timothy 5:18 For the Scriptures says, "Do not muzzle the ox while it is treading out the grain," and "The workers deserves his wages."

❓Question of the day: "Any questions?"

👤 "God created wheat, corn, barley, rye, oats and rice that can be used in breads, pastas and cereals."

○ **AUGUST 11** ○

✏ Little Trooper's liking: "Oatmeal is my favorite food besides milk."

✚ Don't go against the 'grain', unless the 'grain' is heading in the wrong direction!

📖 **Acts 28:3 Paul gathered a pile of brushwood and, as he put it on the fire, a viper, driven out by the heat, fastened itself on his hand.**

❓**Question of the day: "Doesn't this sound mildly phrased?"**

👤 **"It seems to me that boys like mud, snakes, sticks, rocks, worms, sand, lizards, bugs and chocolate chip cookies."**

○AUGUST 12○

👤 **Chew–Chew's question: "Who don't?!"**

✚ **Grandpa does, too!**

📖 **Matthew 7:7 "Ask and it will be given to you; seek and you will find; knock and the door will be opened to you..."**

❓**Question of the day: "Are you ready to ask, seek and knock?"**

🧍 **"I wonder why they don't call 'root beer floats' 'ice cream floats', since the ice cream is what's doing the floating?"**

○ AUGUST 13 ○

🧍 **Baby No-No's concern: "This is what keeps you up at night?"**

✚ **There is no such thing as a stupid question, but sometimes an answer can be considered questionable.**

📖 **John 8:12** When Jesus spoke again to the people, He said, "I am the Light of the world. Whoever follows Me will never walk in darkness, but will have the Light of Life."

❓Question of the day: "Who are you following?"

🧍 "Who likes to run barefoot in the grass? Drag their bare feet through the sand? Dip their bare feet into a swimming pool? Run barefooted across hot pavement to the ice cream stand?"

○AUGUST 14○

✏️ Little Trooper's dream: "I would just like to be able to walk, shoes or no shoes!"

✚ Let Jesus be a light for your path!

📖 **G**enesis 28:12 He had a dream in which he saw a stairway resting on the Earth, with its top reaching to Heaven, and the angels of God were ascending and descending on it.

❓Question of the day: "Do you have dreams like this one?"

🧍 "Bunk beds at the cabin are great fun. They happen to be in the loft, so you will need to climb a ladder to get up there."

○AUGUST 15○

🧍 Lanore's fear: "I fell out of a bunk bed when I was younger and so I think I'll choose to stay on the couch in the den tonight."

✚ Climbing the ladder at any age can be risky business!

📖 **2 Peter 3:9 The Lord is not slow in keeping His promise, as some understand slowness. He is patient with you, not wanting anyone to perish, but everyone to come to repentance.**

❓**Question of the day: "Are we patient with others?"**

🧍 **"Let's play Cat's Cradle! First we will need a long piece of string and then four willing hands. Most importantly...lots and lots of patience."**

○AUGUST 16○

🐈 **Witty Kitty's thought: "It sounds like when Grandpa tries to help one of us get our kite out of a tree in one piece."**

✚ **Longsuffering is a word found in the Bible that means having patience.**

📖 **Romans 16:22 I, Tertius, who wrote down this letter, greet you in the Lord.**

❓Question of the day: "When is the last time you sat down and wrote someone a letter?"

🧍 **"Let's all load up in Grandpa's cart and then he will pull us with his ATV to the mail box for a possible birthday card, anniversary card or a 'just because' letter."**

○AUGUST 17○

🧍 **Chew–Chew's disappointment: "It turned out that we checked the mailbox for 'just because junk mail."**

➕ **Think about someone who would like to receive a handwritten letter from you and then write one.**

📖 **Proverbs 19:9 A false witness will not go unpunished, and he who pours out lies will perish.**

❓**Question of the day: "Isn't this a great reminder to all of us?"**

🕴 "Grandpa fired up his hay wagon to take all of the grandchildren and their parents to see the new water park. It is only visible about two weeks out of the year after the snow melts."

○AUGUST 18○

🕴 Izzy Ann's correction: "Okay, now *that's* an exaggeration!"

✚ White lies are still lies!

📖 **P**salm 115:5-7 They have mouths, but cannot speak, eyes, but they cannot see; they have ears, but cannot hear, noses, but they cannot smell; they have hands, but cannot feel, feet, but they cannot walk; nor can they utter a sound with their throats.

❓Question of the day: "Don't you think that any one of these things would be awful?"

👤 "It's time to give all of you a bath and the pets, too. There...don't you all feel better now?"

○ AUGUST 19 ○

👤 Baby No-No's thought: "I felt fine *before* my bath!"

✝ God created us with a nose to smell with and eyes to see with for a reason.

📖 **P**roverbs 9:9 Instruct a wise man and he will be wiser still; teach a righteous man and he will add to his learning.

❓Question of the day: "Are you willing to add to your learning?"

👤 "We have a loft at the cabin where the grandkiddies like to sleep. They like to climb the ladder to reach it."

○AUGUST 20○

🐕 Fudgy's complaint: "Nobody showed me how to climb a ladder like the circus dogs are trained to do."

✚ True...but can the circus dogs scarf down a colossal box of buttered popcorn and gulp down a liter bottle soda pop like you can?

📖 **Matthew 11:28 Come to me, all you who are weary and burdened, and I will give you rest.**

❓**Question of the day: "Is there anything that feels like a burden to you today?"**

👤 **"Picnic tables are a nice place to sit with your cousins while sipping lemonade, eating frosted oatmeal cookies and playing a couple of rounds of Yahtzee on a lazy summer afternoon."**

○AUGUST 21○

👤 **Mary Lu's observation: "They also provide plenty of shade for the pets to catch a snooze by our feet."**

✚ **Make sure to rest now and then, because if you don't 'come apart' once in a while, you will 'come apart'.**

📖 **Philippians 4:19 And my God will meet all your needs according to His glorious riches in Christ Jesus.**

❓**Question of the day: "What else do we need?"**

👤 **"Being greedy is not something you want your loved ones to remember you by."**

○ AUGUST 22 ○

✏ **Little Trooper's question: "You mean I won't get my allowance doubled next week?"**

✚ **It is not your money anyway...it is God's money. You may have earned it by working for it, but God gave you the gifts and talents to be able to perform the job.**

📖 **1** **Corinthians 2:16 "For who has known the mind of the Lord that he may instruct Him?" But we have the mind of Christ.**

❓Question of the day: "Are you appreciative of this fact?"

🧍 **"Can you name all of the fifty United States of America?...in alphabetical order?... and name their capitols?...I can and it drives me nuts."**

○AUGUST 23○

🧍 **Lanore's suspicion: "I think Grandma has been in the sun a little too long."**

✚ **Being in the boonies helps you get closer to God and His Creation and also gives you plenty of time to let your mind actually think about things.**

📖 **Ecclesiastes 1:5 The sun rises and the sun sets, and hurries back to where it rises.**

❓**Question of the day: "Aren't you totally amazed at this?"**

👤 **"God created the sun and He placed it about 93 million miles away from us so that we have just enough heat from it, yet not have it burn us beyond recognition."**

○ **AUGUST 24** ○

🐱 **Witty Kitty's relief: "I am so glad that God also created the trees to give us shade."**

✝️ **God also provided us with His Son, so we don't burn after this life on Earth!**

📖 **R**omans 15:3 For even Christ did not please Himself but, as it is written: "The insults of those who insult you have fallen on Me."

❓**Question of the day: "What better friend can we have than Jesus?"**

👤 "Throughout our cabin we have lots of painted pictures and enlarged framed photographs hanging on the walls. Grandpa's picture of himself is hung up next to the Wyoming's prairie painting where he longs to be."

○**AUGUST 25**○

🐾 Fudgy's confusion: "Why is there an ice cream stand by the prairie dog town?"

➕ Because even prairie dogs need something to hope for!

📖 **M**atthew 13:13 This is why I speak to them in parables: "Though seeing, they do not see; though hearing, they do not hear or understand..."

❓<u>Question of the day: "Do you understand the parables in the Bible?"</u>

👤 "Whenever Grandpa is away from the cabin all day cutting more firewood to keep us warm, I do not have a pity party. I just pop in an audio tape and either clean, crochet or bake while listening to a story."

○ AUGUST 26 ○

👤 Mary Lu's wish: "I hope that someday I will have a cabin and I can listen to more modern stories."

✚ The Bible is loaded with timeless stories!

📖 Isaiah 12:3 With joy you will draw water from the wells of salvation.

❓Question of the day: "Are you joyful?"

🧍 "I see through my kitchenette's window that Grandpa is filling up the kiddy pool out back. Who would like to go swimming?"

○ AUGUST 27 ○

🧍 🧍 🧍 🧍 🧍 🍼 🐕 🐈 All: "I do! I do! I do! I do! I do! Goo–goo! Woof! Meow!"

✚ Prince Roderick better go to town right quick and buy another pool.

Luke 8:17 For there is nothing hidden that will not be disclosed, and nothing concealed that will not be known or brought out into the open.

?Question of the day: "So why even try to hide it?"

"You should *never* throw a rock, stone, pebble, gravel or even a boulder in the cabin *or* at each other."

☼AUGUST 28☼

Chew–Chew's question: "Can we throw them outside when nobody's around to see us?"

✚ No. Besides...God sees *everything*!

📖 **Revelation 22:8–9** I, John, am the one who heard and saw these things. And when I had heard and seen them, I fell down to worship at the feet of the angel who had been showing them to me. But he said to me, "Do not do it! I am a fellow servant with you and with your brothers the prophets and of all who keep the words of this book. Worship God!"

?Question of the day: "Do you agree that we should worship God always?"

👤 "You can all go to town with me if you promise to act like angels."

☼ AUGUST 29 ☼

👤 Izzy Ann's response: "Where *did* I put those wings?"

✚ Twice in the Book of Revelation an angel told John not to worship him, but to worship God.

📖 Ephesians 4:29 Do not let any unwholesome talk come out of your mouths, but only what is helpful for building others up according to their needs, that it may benefit those who listen.

❓Question of the day: "How are we doing at building other up?"

👤 "Ping–pong is a lot like volleyball, however, if you are short, you have a much better chance to hit the ball, unlike volleyball."

○AUGUST 30○

👤 Baby No–No's conclusion: "Then I ought to play like a professional!"

✚ When carrying on a conversation with someone, play nice. Do not be like the aggressive ping–pong player who tries to slam their opponent between the eyes.

📖 **Joel 2:28** **"And afterward, I will pour out my Spirit on all people. Your sons and daughters will prophesy, your old men will dream dreams, your young men will see visions..."**

❓**Question of the day: "What is your vision for the future?"**

🧍 **"When I pray before I go to sleep, I ask God for sweet dreams. If that is not possible because of a crazy day I just experienced, then I pray that I won't remember my dreams when I awake."**

○AUGUST 31○

🧍 **Mary Lu's prayer: "Please let Grandma Buckskin dream of making us some of her homemade waffles with warm and gooey maple syrup to drizzle over top!"**

✚ **There's a really good chance that will happen, kid.**

📖 **Matthew 4:18–20** As Jesus was walking beside the Sea of Galilee, He saw two brothers, Simon called Peter and his brother Andrew. They were casting a net into the lake, for they were fishermen. "Come, follow Me," Jesus said, "and I will make you fishers of men." At once they left their nets and followed Him.

❓**Question of the day: "How quickly are we willing to drop everything and follow Jesus?"**

👤 "They say that a boat is great for catching a bunch of fish. I sure hope so, because I see that Grandpa forgot the poles again."

🐟 SEPTEMBER 1 🐟

👤 Kimberella's remark: "Luckily, he remembered a fishing net to go about it the old fashioned way."

✚ Remember when you have a choice between right or left and right or wrong... always choose to be 'right'!

📖 **Joshua 1:9 "...Have I not commanded you? Be strong and courageous. Do not be terrified; do not be discouraged, for the Lord your God will be with you wherever you go."**

❓**Question of the day: "Are you strong or terrified?"**

🧍 **"Let's talk about sliding boards! They can be high and steep; made of metal; made of plastic; curvy; go through a tunnel; short and fast; side by side; leading into a pool; made for a gunny sack; connected to a boat and even used as a way to exit a plane in case of an emergency."**

🐿️ SEPTEMBER 2 🐿️

🧍 **Baby No–No's plea: "Stop talking about slides and please take me to one!"**

➕ **May you never get shocked, burned, dizzy, scared of heights, pushed down or have an emergency!**

📖 **Proverbs 13:3** He who scorns instruction will pay for it, but he who respects a command is rewarded.

❓**Question of the day: "Are you willing to take a command?"**

👤 "I always seem to be reminding our grandchildren to zip up their coats before running laps around the field behind the barn."

🐿 SEPTEMBER 3 🐿

👤 Chew–Chew's thoughts: "Zippers are handy for suitcases, backpacks, clothing, purses and pencil pouches...right up to the time one or two teeth go missing and then they are classified as junk."

✚ The best kind of a zipper may be the invisible one for our mouths when we are tempted to say something that we should not.

📖 **Proverbs 12:18 Reckless words pierce like a sword, but the tongue of the wise brings healing.**

❓**Question of the day: "Do your words cut or soothe?"**

👤 **"Fudgy is a dog, pet *and* friend to me."**

🐾 SEPTEMBER 4 🐾

👤 **Prince Roderick's claim: "I like Fudgy when he behaves himself. In other words about two percent of the time."**

✚ **If you don't have anything nice to say, then please don't. That goes for dogs, too!**

📖 **L**uke 1:31 You will be with child and give birth to a son, and you are to give Him the name Jesus.

?Question of the day: "Can you imagine having an angel telling you this?"

👤 "Our neighboring farmer couple are expecting their first child, so I asked if any of my granddaughters could come along with me to the baby shower. The invitation said they are expecting a girl. Grandpa Buckskin can't stand it when the baby's sex is announced before the birth."

🐿 SEPTEMBER 5 🐿

👤 Mary Lu's observation: "Mary and Joseph knew before Jesus was born that they were going to have a son and what they were going to name Him. That was over two thousand years ago!"

✝ And we think *we* are 'in the know' this day and age!

📖 **Psalm 62:5 Find rest, O my soul, in God alone; my hope comes from Him.**

❓Question of the day: "Is your hope in God?"

👤 "I think that quiet time is very important so young and old alike can pray, think and rest."

🐿 SEPTEMBER 6 🐿

👤 Lanore's suggestion: "A hammock among the trees, a lawn chair in the grass, a comfy chair by the fireplace or a stump in the woods are the best places to do so."

✚ To be able to hear what the Holy Spirit is trying to tell you, you must turn down *or* turn off the noise.

📖 **2 Thessalonians 3:10 For even when we were with you, we gave you this rule: "If a man will not work, he shall not eat."**

❓**Question of the day: "Doesn't this sound like a sensible rule?"**

👤 "It is Labor Day to honor those who work outside or inside the home. Children, please raise the flag high on the pole!"

🐿️ SEPTEMBER 7 🐿️

🐱 Witty Kitty's tribute: "Thank you Grandpa for earning a salary that helps me have food in my bowl every day!"

➕ Please thank your parents, spouses and anyone who helps contribute to your home running like a clock...better get back to work!

📖 **E**xodus 34:1 The Lord said to Moses, "Chisel out two stone tablets like the first ones, and I will write on them the words that were on the first tablets, which you broke.

?Question of the day: "Did you know that there were two sets of the Ten Commandments?"

👤 "Kids, did you know that God had Moses write the Ten Commandments on the original two tablets, then Moses smashed them to the ground and God ended up rewriting them on two other tablets?"

🐿 SEPTEMBER 8 🐿

👤 Chew–Chew's comparison: "My Uncle Jack broke a horse shoe once...make that twice!"

✚ The Ten Commandments' tablets were placed in the Ark of the Covenant.

📖 **Habakkuk 2:5** Indeed, wine betrays him; he is arrogant and never at rest. Because he is greedy as the grave and like death is never satisfied, he gathers to himself all the nations and takes captive all the peoples.

❓**Question of the day: "Doesn't it seem like there is never a time to be greedy?"**

👤 "Grandpa knows that most people really don't want another s'more. They really want to sit around the campfire and politely eat every last chocolate bar you have on hand."

🐿 SEPTEMBER 9 🐿

👤 Lanore's pondering: "Maybe they should rename the outside treat 's'nough'."

✚ Moderation is the key and chocolate bars are very tempting!

📖 **1 Corinthians 6:11 And that is what some of you were. But you were washed, you were sanctified in the Name of the Lord Jesus Christ and by the Spirit of our God.**

❓**Question of the day: "Are you washed and sanctified?"**

🚹 **"I think that taking a bath at our cabin can be considered a sport. One has to get the water from the well, heat it up on the stove, pour it into the tub little by little and be quick enough to have your turn in line so the water is still warm."**

🐾 SEPTEMBER 10 🐾

🚹 **Prince Roderick's discovery: "This is where the phrase 'Don't throw the baby out with the bathwater' comes into play. In other words...the water is so dirty that you can't see the baby."**

✚ **Whatever happened to 'Women and children first'?**

📖 **John 4:23 Yet a time is coming and has now come when the true worshipers will worship the Father in spirit and truth, for they are the kind of worshipers the Father seeks.**

❓**Question of the day: "Don't we all want to be the kind of worshiper that God is seeking?"**

🧍 **"Whether you see the American flag flying high or at half–staff, please be respectful of it."**

🐿 SEPTEMBER 11 🐿

🧍 **Izzy Ann's request: "Please let us have the Pledge of Allegiance back in our schools. We need it!"**

✚ **Do not *worship* the flag, save your worshiping for God!**

📖 **Revelation 19:10** ...at this I fell at his feet to worship him. But he said to me, "Do not do it! I am a fellow servant with you and with your brothers who hold to the testimony of Jesus. Worship God! For the testimony of Jesus is the Spirit of Prophecy."

❓**Question of the day: "Did you read the whole Book of Revelation yet?"**

👤 "Speaking of worshiping things that are not God, include animals on your list. God created them for our enjoyment, but they aren't humans or better than humans...they are animals."

🐀 SEPTEMBER 12 🐀

🐱 Witty Kitty's comment: "Yes Fudgy... this mean you, too!"

✚ Do not worship another human being either.

📖 **2 Corinthians 9:15 Thanks be to God for His indescribable gift!**

❓<u>Question of the day</u>: "<u>Are you thankful?</u>"

🚶 **"I think that celebrating Grandparents' Day is unnecessary. If we are lucky enough to be one, then we are lucky enough!"**

🐾 SEPTEMBER 13 🐾

✏️ **Little Trooper's two cents worth: "All of my grandparents are *my* present!"**

✚ **Please acknowledge your grandparents throughout the year.**

📖 **D**euteronomy 22:5 A woman must not wear men's clothing, nor a man wear women's clothing, for the Lord your God detests anyone who does this.

❓<u>Question of the day: "Doesn't this about sum this subject up?"</u>

👤 "Grandpa knows that girls consist of butterflies, clean hands, dresses, flowers, bunnies and snow cones."

🐿 SEPTEMBER 14 🐿

👤 Baby No–No's conclusion: "There goes the clean hands and dresses."

✚ God made males and females differently for a reason. His reason.

📖 **S**ong of Songs 2:3 Like an apple tree among the trees of the forest is my lover among the young men. I delight to sit in his shade, and his fruit is sweet to my taste.

?Question of the day: "Did you eat an apple today?"

🧍 "Hey kids, can you please pick me a bushel of apples off of that tree over yonder? Then I will be able to make you all a hot apple pie this afternoon and we can enjoy caramel apples tomorrow."

🐚 SEPTEMBER 15 🐚

🧍 Mary Lu's dream: "I hope Grandma will make at least two caramel apples for each of us."

✚ May all of your dreams be sweet, but not *too* sweet!

📖 **Proverbs 22:15 Folly is bound up in the heart of a child, but the rod of discipline will drive it far from him.**

❓**Question of the day: "Who agrees that discipline isn't always easy?"**

👤 **"Grandpa and I do not allow tantrums · to be thrown in our cabin. Period."**

🐿 SEPTEMBER 16 🐿

👤 **Chew–Chew's warning: "Please don't throw *anything* in their cabin!"**

➕ **The best way to get someone's attention is be the politest kid on the block...or field.**

📖 **Matthew 25:8 The foolish ones said to the wise, 'Give us some of your oil; our lamps are going out.'**

❓**Question of the day: "Are you prepared?"**

🧍 "If you are lucky enough to celebrate your birthday at the cabin, then you will be given either a special hat or a tiara to wear."

🐿 SEPTEMBER 17 🐿

🐈 Fudgy's complaint: "Grandma never lets me blow out her candles and lately she doesn't even *have* candles on her cake."

✚ Always keep your lantern trimmed for Jesus!

📖 **Psalm 139:13 For You created my inmost being; you knit me together in my mother's womb.**

❓**Question of the day: "Do you find yourself speechless sometimes?"**

🧍 **"There is just something about sitting on the front porch and working with yarn. Now where is my iced tea and windmill cookies?"**

🐈 SEPTEMBER 18 🐈

🐈 **Witty Kitty's wish: "Why, oh, why can't one of those fun balls of yarn drop off of Grandma's lap?"**

✚ **Don't wish your life away, for it is precious!**

📖 **P**roverbs 16:19 In his heart a man plans his course, but the Lord determines his steps.

?Question of the day: "Are you flexible with your plans in case they get changed?"

👤 "At the one–room school house near us, recess comes in between learning. At our cabin the kiddies learn things *during* recess."

🐸 SEPTEMBER 19 🐸

👤 Lanore's observation: "This is why Grandma and Grandpa Buckskin are not allowed to home school us. Ever!"

✚ There is a time and a place for everything and God has a plan for everyone, even though we think we know best.

📖 **Proverbs 27:17 As iron sharpens iron, so one man sharpens another.**

❓Question of the day: "Doesn't it sound kind of dull to be a loner?"

🚶 **"It looks like Grandpa is starting his dream project that is a miniature golf course in the corn field. He wants to have each hole represent a state in this great nation of ours."**

🐾 SEPTEMBER 20 🐾

✏️ **Little Trooper's thought: "That would be a very long game."**

✚ **Better take your 'iron' – you're going to need it!**

📖 **P**hilippians 3:19 Their destiny is destruction, their god is their stomach, and their glory is in their shame. Their mind is on earthly things.

?Question of the day: "Where are our minds at this moment?"

⛊ "Do you remember the time that I ran out of cookies? I don't either."

🐿 SEPTEMBER 21 🐿

⛊ Baby No–No's memory: "Remember the time when Grandpa had that really bad tummy ache and he had to be driven by horses to the doctor? Remember?"

✚ Eating until your heart's content doesn't mean that your stomach will feel the same.

📖 **Jeremiah 17:8 "...He will be like a tree planted by the water that sends out its roots by the stream. It does not fear when heat comes; its leaves are always green. It has no worries in a year of drought and never fails to bear fruit."**

❓Question of the day: "Have you visited a creek in your neck of the woods lately?"

🧍 **"Autumn is such a beautiful season! The leaves are spectacular and the days and nights are cooler. I need to go find my sweater."**

🐁 SEPTEMBER 22 🐁

🐈 **Witty Kitty's daydream: "Apple cider, maple syrup, raking leaves, flannel shirts, mice moving in..."**

✝ **God created autumn for us to enjoy. Please don't waste the season away by dreading the winter that will follow.**

Habakkuk 2:2 Then the Lord replied: "Write down the revelation and make it plain on tablets so that a herald may run with it..."

?Question of the day: "Does anyone have a pen?"

"I have found that the best way to write is to get out a spiral notebook and go for it."

SEPTEMBER 23

Mary Lu's advice: "Make sure to set a timer, because once you're on a roll, you can't stop doing it!"

✚ God had many men write the Bible and they were all inspired by Him.

📖 **Luke 8:23–25 As they sailed, He fell asleep. A squall came down on the lake, so that the boat was being swamped, and they were in great danger. The disciples went and woke Him, saying, "Master, Master, we're going to drown!" He got up and rebuked the wind and the raging waters; the storm subsided, and all was calm. "Where is your faith?" He asked His disciples. In fear and amazement they asked one another, "Who is this? He commands even the winds and the water, and they obey Him."**

?Question of the day: "Where is your faith in the storms of your life?"

👤 **"We don't have a basement at our cabin, however Grandpa installed a door that will lead us underground in case of a tornado."**

🐾 SEPTEMBER 24 🐾

🐕 **Fudgy's worry: "I hope they remember to take me down there, too. Poor Toto!"**

✝ **Trust God *and* seek shelter when a bad storm is coming or predicted to come!**

📖 **Mark 16:15** He said to them, "Go into all the world and preach the Good News to all Creation..."

❓**Question of the day: "How are we doing on this one?"**

👤 "If I were a teacher I would like the children to leave a caramel apple on my desk from time–to–time. With lots of peanuts, please."

🐌 SEPTEMBER 25 🐌

👤 Izzy Ann's conclusion: "Get back to reality, Grandma!"

✚ The best gift you can give someone is sharing the Gospel with them!

📖 **E**cclesiastes 4:10 If one falls down, his friend can help him up. But pity the man who falls and has no one to help him up!

❓**Question of the day: "Do you have someone like this to help you?"**

🧍 "Sharing can be fun. Who would like some of my king–size candy bar? Anyone? Well, at least I tried."

🐰 SEPTEMBER 26 🐰

🧍 Prince Roderick's advice: "Next time you might want to get out of the broom closet so the kids and I can hear you."

✚ It is way more fun to observe God's Creation like Niagara Falls or the Grand Canyon with another pair of eyes!

📖 **Job 14:7** "At least there is hope for a tree: If it is cut down, it will sprout again, and its new shoots will not fail..."

❓**Question of the day: "Doesn't it sound like cutting trees are a good thing?"**

👤 "I see Grandpa is heading for the woods to cut down dead trees. I better make some apple crisp for a treat when he's done working so hard all morning."

🐿 SEPTEMBER 27 🐿

👤 Chew–Chew's knowledge: "Trees can be used for firewood, paper, cardboard, boxes, telephone poles, etc."

✚ If you cut down trees for a living, please replant some for the future!

📖 **M**alachi 3:10 "...Bring the whole tithe into the storehouse, that there may be food in My house. Test me in this," says the Lord Almighty, "and see if I will not throw open the floodgates of Heaven and pour out so much blessing that you will not have room enough for it...."

❓Question of the day: "Can we say, 'Wow!'?"

👤 "How many times do you hear anyone telling you that it is okay to throw rocks? At our cabin in the sticks, you will hear it quite often, but only to skip them across the pond out back."

🐸 **SEPTEMBER 28** 🐸

👤 Baby No–No's guess: "Grandpa will be the one who will have the most skips, because he is much stronger than the rest of us."

✚ There is a sale on windows at Big World Shopping Center for another week.

📖 **P**salm 89:37 "...it will be established Forever like the moon, the faithful witness in the sky."

❓**Question of the day: "Isn't it cool that the moon is a faithful witness?"**

🧍 "Hello Mr. Moon! Are you 'full'? Are you 'half'? Are you 'new'? Maybe just a 'quarter', 'waxing' or 'waning'? Any way you are – you were created by God Almighty!"

🐿 SEPTEMBER 29 🐿

🧍 Kimberella's remarks: "The moon, whether seen or unseen on a given night, gives us gravity and makes the tides in the ocean."

✚ Let there be light!

📖 **John 1:5 The light shines in the darkness, but the darkness has not understood it.**

❓**Question of the day: "Are you being a shining light to someone?"**

👤 **"Why is it when you are in need of a flashlight, it is not where you last put it? Prince Roderick...where are you?!"**

🐇 SEPTEMBER 30 🐇

🔦 **Little Trooper's answer: "When the lights come back on, the mystery of the missing flashlight will be solved."**

✚ **A place for everything and everything in its place. It may be time to take down the Bible off that dusty book shelf so it can be seen and therefore, read!**

📖 **2 Thessalonians 3:13 And as for you, brothers, never tire of doing what is right.**

❓Question of the day: "Don't you think that maybe it would be more tiring to be doing things that are wrong?"

🚹 "I like to use a strip of Velcro to hang reminder notes all over the cabin. Now I need a note to tell me where I keep the Velcro."

☾ OCTOBER 1 ☾

🚹 Izzy Ann's experience: "If Velcro doesn't make the sound that can rip you right out of bed, then it's probably worn out and won't stick to itself anymore."

✚ Don't be 'worn out' as a Christian. Please get out there and get someone stuck on Jesus!

📖 **1 Peter 4:9 Offer hospitality to one another without grumbling. Hebrews 13:2 Do not forget to entertain strangers, for by doing so some people have entertained angels without knowing it.**

❓<u>**Question of the day: "Do you ever wonder if you have seen an angel and didn't even know it?"**</u>

👤 **"We have a pet bird that can say quite a few words and phrases. One of them is: 'Y'all come back now!'"**

☾ OCTOBER 2 ☾

🐈 **Fudgy's excuse: "That's why I can never get past the front porch."**

➕ **Be hospitable to everyone who enters your home and even those who live there. What a concept!**

📖 **1** Peter 3:22 ...who has gone into Heaven and is at God's Right Hand – with angels, authorities and powers in submission to Him.

❓<u>Question of the day: "Isn't this awesome?"</u>

🧍 "Jesus Christ was resurrected and He is seated at the Right Hand of God Almighty. When we accept Jesus into our lives and are willing to live for Him, we will someday be raised up to be with Him for all Eternity!"

☾ OCTOBER 3 ☾

🧍 Lanore's response: "Halleluiah!"

✝ Please don't wait another day, hour or even minute. The time is *now* if you haven't accepted Jesus Christ as your Savior!

📖 **C**olossians 3:17 And whatever you do, whether in word or deed, do it all in the Name of the Lord Jesus, giving thanks to God the Father through Him.

❓**Question of the day:** "What would our world be like it everyone followed this advice?"

🚹 "Time for supper! Can someone please ring the dinner bell on the back porch? We are having fried chicken, mashed potatoes and gravy, corn on the cob, vegetables from the garden, and a glass of ice cold milk."

☾ **OCTOBER 4** ☾

🚹 Mary Lu's hope: "Please let there be warm brownies and ice cream for dessert."

✚ No matter what is being served, a prayer before devouring it is appropriate.

📖 **2 John 1:7** Many deceivers, who do not acknowledge Jesus Christ as coming in the flesh, have gone out into the world. Any such person is the deceiver and the antichrist.

❓Question of the day: "Are you aware of any deceivers?"

🕴 "Speaking of bells...I think I hear the school bell from the one–room school house way over yonder. I think pranksters ring it once a day just to scare the children within earshot to think they are late even though the school has been closed for years."

☾ OCTOBER 5 ☾

🐱 Witty Kitty's wit: "They must be the same people who rattle an empty bag of cat treats just to see me run."

✚ Do not be tricked. Read the Book of Revelation to know the difference between the real Jesus and the antichrist. The latter will not go by that name and will do his very best to trick many people into thinking that he is the one they are waiting for.

📖 **James 5:16 Therefore, confess your sins to each other and pray for each other so that you may be healed. The prayer of a righteous man is powerful and effective.**

❓**Question of the day: "Do you or someone else you know need healing?"**

🚶 **"Today is the National Day of Prayer. Here at the cabin we like to pray not only for our nation, but for the whole world."**

☾ OCTOBER 6 ☾

🚶 **Mary Lu's thought: "Please don't wait an entire year to pray for others. Pray every day."**

✝ **Even though God has everything under control, the answer to, 'Why pray then?' is this: Prayer lets us give our worries and anxieties to God and shows our faith in Him that we know He is in charge, which in turn gives us peace. It can also make us recognize our needs and that they can only be met with God's Divine Intervention!**

📖 **P**salm 118:24 This is the day the Lord has made; let us rejoice and be glad in it.

❓**Question of the day: "Are you rejoicing?"**

👤 "The dentist recommends that you brush your teeth two to three times a day (and floss.) I recommend that if you are staying with me for the next few days, make sure that you make it four times a day. I have plenty of time slots that have a snack as part of the program."

☾ OCTOBER 7 ☾

👤 Baby No–No's complaint: "No fair! I don't have teeth to brush *or* to eat snacks with...wah!!"

✚ Don't rush it kid. You will cut some baby teeth in and eventually they will all fall out right before school pictures are taken. Then you will cut in some wisdom teeth and they will more than likely become impacted and have to be taken out sometime in your teenage years right before prom. You will have a few decades of visits to the dentist to fill old cavities, build bridges, get crowned, replace old crowns, lose a permanent tooth and need to rebuild a bridge or have an implant. This will all be in vain, because when you are very old, you will probably have to have all your teeth pulled and go toothless for a few months before you get fake ones put in and find it hard to eat your favorite snacks anyway.

📖 **Genesis 1:27 So God Created man in His own image, in the image of God He created him; male and female He created them.**

❓Question of the day: "Is it just me or does it sound like God is driving home a point in this verse?"

🧍 **"God created mankind. All the races are just a variation of mankind. Woman is mankind. There is one race...you guessed it... the human race."**

☾ OCTOBER 8 ☾

🧍 **Izzy Ann's reminder: "And let us not forget the mannequin!"**

✚ **God created everything and everyone the way He saw fit. We are different on the outside and the inside for a reason. Let's celebrate this fact!**

📖 **2** Peter 2:22 "...Of them, the proverbs are true: A dog returns to its vomit," and, "A sow that is washed goes back to her wallowing in the mud."

❓Question of the day: "Are you returning to a bad habit?"

🧍 "It's laundry day! Children, please gather up all of your clothes that need washing on this beautiful sunny day. Sort the whites from the colors and the ordinary dirty from the extremely filthy. After they are washed, we will eat Popsicles outside while I hang the items on the clothes line."

☽ OCTOBER 9 ☽

🧍 Chew–Chew's reality: "All of my clothes got put into one pile...muddy brown. Grandpa showed me a good time on the four–wheeler after that storm we had the other day. A few times."

✚ Please help your parents and grandparents out by taking care of your clothes!

📖 **Luke 21:18 But not a hair of your head will perish.**

❓**Question of the day: "So...what are you worried about?"**

👤 **"This time of year makes all of us want to get out our hooded sweatshirts. I cut mine off last year because the thing messed up my hair. I guess now that I have no hood, the forty mile per hour winds will make it even messier. Where *is* my hat?!"**

☾ OCTOBER 10 ☾

👤 **Lanore's confusion: "I never have seen Grandma's hair messed up. It looks the same all the time."**

➕ **When words are many, sin is not absent.**

📖 **1** **Timothy 5:8 If anyone does not provide for his relatives, and especially for his immediate family, he has denied the faith and is worse than an unbeliever.**

❓**Question of the day: "Are we providing for our relatives in need?"**

👤 **"Whether someone is your first, second or even third cousin, they are related to you no matter what."**

☾ OCTOBER 11 ☾

✏️ **Little Trooper's observation: "Everyone is related to each other all the way back to Noah."**

✝️ **This is why prejudice is just silly. It was sparked by Evolution. No one is better than anyone else. We are all sinners and we all need Jesus Christ as our Savior!**

📖 **J**eremiah 33:3 'Call to Me and I will answer you and tell you great and unsearchable things you do not know.'

❓Question of the day: "When is the last time you called out to God?"

🧍 "Okay kids...listen up! Grandpa is going to give you a fact of history."

🧍 "In 1492, Columbus sailed the ocean blue."

☾ OCTOBER 12 ☾

🧍 Kimberella's ponder: "If it were the year 1493, it would give the poet a chance to be able to use the word 'sea'."

✚ Tough break.

📖 **P**roverbs 7:4 "...say to wisdom, "You are my sister," and call understanding your kinsman;..."

?Question of the day: "Have you asked for wisdom and understanding?"

🧍 Someday kiddies, you will grow up and your wisdom teeth will decide to make an appearance."

☾ OCTOBER 13 ☾

🐈 Fudgy's interruption: "If you are lucky, you can keep them for the rest of your life."

✚ Pray for wisdom and understanding. That wisdom will be your sister and understanding be your kinsman.

📖 **James 1:26** If anyone considers himself religious and yet does not keep a tight rein on his tongue, he deceives himself and his religion is worthless.

❓**Question of the day: "Is our reins tight or slack?"**

🧍 "Grandpa tends to call any child under the age of twelve a 'yard ape'. This is why his yard includes monkey bars."

☾ OCTOBER 14 ☾

🐱 Witty Kitty's warning: "Watch your tongue on those frigid days!"

✚ Everyone should watch their tongue during every waking hour!

📖 **Proverbs 29:11** A fool gives full vent to his anger, but a wise man keeps himself under control.

❓**Question of the day: "Do we want to be wise today or fools?"**

👤 "Our property supposedly has a cave on the back left corner of it."

☾ OCTOBER 15 ☾

🐈 Fudgy's memory: "That is just a hole in the side of a hill to store the potatoes in a cool place."

✚ Don't lose your cool and become a hot potato, otherwise you could end up living in a cave!

📖 **Luke 1:41** When Elizabeth heard Mary's greeting, the baby leaped in her womb, and Elizabeth was filled with the Holy Spirit.

?Question of the day: "Wouldn't this be a great experience?"

🧍 "Grandpa and I think that if a child is face–to–face with a stranger that is just trying to say 'hello' and the child is with another adult, then they should say 'hello' back to them."

☾ **OCTOBER 16** ☾

🧍 Baby No–No's know: "Of course if you are *not* with another adult, like your parent, then you should be very careful!"

✚ This goes for adults too...especially when social media is pretending to be someone they are not!

📖 **Joshua 1:9 "...Have I not commanded you? Be strong and courageous. Do not be terrified; do not be discouraged, for the Lord your God will be with you wherever you go."**

❓**Question of the day: "Are you terrified of something?"**

🚹 **"At our cabin, the only stranger you will see is a scarecrow in the cornfield next door."**

☾ OCTOBER 17 ☾

🐱 **Witty Kitty's alert: "It's time to replace that raggedy guy since the birds built that big nest of theirs on top of his hat and made him topple over."**

✚ **Don't be scared...God is with you!**

📖 **Ephesians 5:4 Nor should there be obscenity, foolish talk or coarse joking, which are out of place, but rather thanksgiving.**

❓**Question of the day: "Do you listen to bad jokes or excuse yourself from the conversation?"**

🧍 **"What is the difference between a frog and a toad?" (Answer is: Warts!)**

☾ OCTOBER 18 ☾

🧍 **Prince Roderick's riddle: "What is the difference between a wart and a mole?" (Answer is: A wart is a pesky bump on top your skin and a mole is a pest that lives under the ground!)**

✚ **Never mind.**

📖 **Romans 15:13 May the God of hope fill you with all joy and peace as you trust in Him, so that you may overflow with hope by the power of the Holy Spirit.**

❓**Question of the day: "Do you have hope?"**

👤 "I just love a campfire! That makes me think...without a campfire there wouldn't be s'mores. Without s'mores there wouldn't be Girl Scouts. Without Girl Scouts, there wouldn't be cookies. Without cookies, there wouldn't be milk involved to dunk them in. Without milk, there wouldn't be any cheese. Without 'cheese', no pictures would be taken. Without pictures, there wouldn't be any evidence of how many s'mores I *really* ate while distracting everyone with my rambling on. I just *love* a campfire!"

☾ OCTOBER 19 ☾

👤 Izzy Ann's hope: "I want to stay a 'Brownie' forever!"

✚ Without Jesus, there *is* no hope!

📖 **R**omans 15:7 Accept one another, then, just as Christ accepted you, in order to bring praise to God.

❓Question of the day: "Is there someone we can accept into our lives?"

🚹 **"I think that gym class (or P.E. for you technical folks) could be fun if they would do away with the assigned standard gym suit."**

☾ OCTOBER 20 ☾

🚹 **Lanore's excitement: "At Grandma and Grandpa Buckskin's cabin, our gym class consists of a jungle gym, T-ball, hiking, Frisbee, skipping though the fields and rope climbing."**

✚ **Where do I sign up?**

📖 **P**roverbs 31:30 Charm is deceptive, and beauty is fleeting; but a woman who fears the Lord is to be praised.

❓Question of the day: "Do you fear the Lord?"

🧍 "What is your favorite costume? Oh, I guess you are wearing it...don't tell me.... ummm..."

☽ OCTOBER 21 ☾

🧍 Chew–Chew's beef: "I'm not wearing one...these are my pajamas, Grandma!"

✚ Beauty is more than skin deep!

📖 **1 Peter 3:15–16 But in your hearts set apart Christ as Lord. Always be prepared to give an answer to everyone who asks you to give the reason for the hope that you have. But do this with gentleness and respect, keeping a clear conscience, so that those who speak maliciously against your good behavior in Christ may be ashamed of their slander.**

?Question of the day: "Do you have your answer ready when someone asks you?"

🧍 **"Horsey swings are fun to ride for something different on our cabin's back porch."**

☾ OCTOBER 22 ☾

🧍 **Mary Lu's complaint: "I wish they could design them so the chain in the back doesn't go up your spine into the back of your head. It feels like you are in the middle of a stickup."**

✚ **Don't be stuck up. Be prepared to share with someone the hope that *you* have!**

📖 **P**roverbs 15:1 A gentle answer turns away wrath, but a harsh word stirs up anger.

❓<u>Question of the day</u>: <u>"Do we tend to be gentle or harsh when speaking to others?"</u>

👤 "If there is one thing that I just can't tolerate, it's bickering. To me it's equal to a car door that is left open while Grandpa is shutting the gate and the warning bell keeps dinging for ten minutes. It is also equal to an alarm clock going off that Grandpa set and is taking an extra-long shower so I have to be the one to crawl over to the noise maker and shut it off or listen to it for a half an hour. Then when I finally reach the contraption, Mr. Buckskin comes in the bedroom fully dressed and says, 'Good morning Doll, why are you up so early?!'"

☾ OCTOBER 23 ☾

👤 Prince Roderick's stab: "It sounds to me like there is actually three things you can't seem to tolerate."

➕ Four, actually.

📖 **1 John 2:15 Do not love the world or anything in the world. If anyone loves the world, the love of the Father is not in him.**

❓Question of the day: "Do you love the world or do you know that you are a citizen of Heaven and just live in this world for the time being?"

🧍 "We have a globe that is kept in the corner by the fireplace in our front room of the cabin. Grandpa likes to use it when the news is on the radio to see where they are talking about. I, on the other hand, like to use it to plan on making my *own* news on a future trip."

☾ OCTOBER 24 ☾

🐈 **Witty Kitty's plan: "When they aren't in the room, I like to knock the thing over and bat it around like a ball of yarn."**

✚ **The cat is out of the bag now!**

📖 **P**salm 147:4 He determines the number of stars and calls them each by name.

❓Question of the day: "Did you know that God has every star named?"

👤 "Boys and girls, can you please name all of the planets in our Milky Way?"

☾ OCTOBER 25 ☾

✐ Little Trooper's answer: "Earth, Jupiter, Mars, Mercury, Neptune, Uranus, Saturn and Venus."

✚ Very good! You listed them in alphabetical order! My grandkids are geniuses...just sayin'.

📖 **Romans 15:4 For everything that was written in the past was written to teach us, so that through endurance and the encouragement of the Scriptures we might have hope.**

❓Question of the day: "Isn't it clear that the Bible was well thought out?"

🧍 **"Grandpa went down the road a piece and rounded up six donkeys for all of you grandkiddies to ride on this afternoon."**

☾ OCTOBER 26 ☾

🐾 **Fudgy's input: "I think their names are: Sandy, Candy, Randy, Mandy, Andy and Dandy. That way they will all respond to commands at the exact same time."**

✚ **That's handy. So is a pocket-size Bible!**

📖 **2 Chronicles 2:7** "Send me, therefore, a man skilled to work in gold and silver, bronze and iron, and in purple, crimson and blue yarn, and experienced in the art of engraving, to work in Judah and Jerusalem with my skilled craftsmen, whom my father, David provided..."

❓Question of the day: "What are your skills?"

👤 "What is your favorite color? Mine is pink."

☾ OCTOBER 27 ☾

👤 Chew–Chew's choice: "All of them."

✝ In Heaven we might be able to hear the colors. Who knows? God knows.

📖 **Luke 12:34 For where your treasure is, there your heart will be also.**

❓**Question of the day: "Are your treasures here on Earth or are they being stored up in Heaven?"**

👤 **"Hey everybody! It's getting to the end of October, which means we need to rake up all the leaves that fell so far. It's interesting that most households have more than one rake, isn't it?"**

☾ OCTOBER 28 ☾

👤 **Mary Lu's conclusion: "Grandpa must really be interesting since he has ten rakes."**

✚ **Many hands make light work and many rakes can clog up the back shed.**

📖 **P**salm 107:1 Give thanks to the Lord, for He is good; His love endures Forever.

❓**Question of the day: "What more is there to say?"**

🧍 "Watch this! 'You're IT!' Those are two little words that can turn a bunch of bored children into a squealing, energized mob for about a half an hour."

☾ OCTOBER 29 ☾

🧍 Izzy Ann's comparison: "Kind of like when we hear Grandma pull a cookie sheet out of the oven with the first batch of warm, gooey chocolate chips cookies on it."

✚ Always remember to say 'Thank you' every time you are handed a cookie or anything else!

📖 **M**ark 13:18-19 Pray that this will not take place in winter, because those will be days of distress unequaled from the beginning, when God created the world, until now – and never to be equaled again.

❓<u>**Question of the day: "Doesn't this sound serious?"**</u>

🧍 **"Halloween at the Buckskins' cabin means bobbing for apples, dressing up as pioneers, hay wagon rides, picking Indian corn, drinking apple cider, carving pumpkins and lots and lots of giggling."**

☾ **OCTOBER 30** ☾

🧍 **Kimberella's confession: "From too much candy."**

✝ **Enjoy each season the day it arrives until the very last day. Then brace yourself for the next one!**

📖 **John 14:6 Jesus answered, "I am the way and the truth and the life. No one comes to the Father except through Me."**

❓**Question of the day: "Got it?"**

"Trick or Treat is a little bit different out where we live. The neighbors are too far apart to go door-to-door, so we have our grandchildren go tree-to-tree."

☾ OCTOBER 31 ☾

Baby No–No's excitement: "Last year we picked apples, then tree nuts, then plums, then pears, then tapped into some maple syrup!"

✝ **Truth can be stranger than fiction!**

📖 **Revelation 14:12** **This calls for patient endurance on the part of the saints who obey God's Commandments and remain faithful to Jesus.**

❓**Question of the day: "Are you a patient saint?"**

🚹 **"There's a church in the valley by the wild wood...wait! That's a song, but there really *is* one there in our neck of the woods."**

🍽 NOVEMBER 1 🍽

🚹 **Lanore's reminder: "Today is All Saints' Day."**

✚ **The 'church' is not a building. It consists of believers in Jesus Christ!**

📖 **Ephesians 4:28 He who has been stealing must steal no longer, but must work, doing something useful with his own hands, that he may have something to share with those in need.**

❓**Question of the day: "Are we doing things that are useful?"**

🧍 **"Did you know that tennis shoes are great for playing sports? Of course you do... but did you know that at our cabin, picking up sticks to start a campfire is considered a sport?"**

🍽 NOVEMBER 2 🍽

✏️ **Little Trooper's question: "Is it because there are two spectators (not naming names) on lawn chairs that qualify it as such?"**

➕ **Please don't be just a spectator. Get involved in *something*. You'll be glad you did and so will the people that you make an impact on. It doesn't *have* to be a sport.**

📖 **James 1:19–20 My dear brothers, take note of this: Everyone should be quick to listen, slow to speak and slow to become angry, for man's anger does not bring about the righteous life that God desires.**

?Question of the day: "How are we doing on this?"

👤 **"Grandpa says that a pet turtle is a lot of fun *if* you're not in a hurry when you call its name or while watching it grow."**

🍽️ NOVEMBER 3 🍽️

👤 **Prince Roderick's warning: "Snakes absolutely love them!"**

➕ **Remember QSS – Quick to listen, Slow to speak, Slow to get angry!**

📖 **Galatians 2:20 I have been crucified with Christ and I no longer live, but Christ lives in me. The life I live in the body, I live by faith in the Son of God, who loved me and gave Himself for me.**

❓**Question of the day: "Are you living for Christ?"**

👤 **"I wonder who thought to make a jigsaw puzzle in the first place? Did a person paint a picture of a farm scene, go to their shed and build themselves a machine that cuts one hundred to two thousand different shaped pieces, cut the beautiful painting up, spend another week or so assembling the pieces back into a farm scene, stand back and say, 'Now *that's* more like it, now where *is* my glue bottle?'"**

🍽 NOVEMBER 4 🍽

👤 **Baby No–No's statement: "I'm just glad someone *did* think of it. I happen to *like* puzzles!"**

✚ **If you feel like *peace* is missing from your life – fill in the hole with a Jesus shaped *piece*!**

📖 **P**roverbs 23:20–21 Do not join those who drink too much wine or gorge themselves on meat, for drunkards and gluttons become poor and drowsiness clothes them in rags.

?<u>Question of the day: "Do you join in or use self-control?"</u>

🕴 "Wake up kiddies! It's breakfast time! Grandpa is outside over the campfire making pan–fried eggs, sausage on a stick, toast and cowboy coffee. I'm going to make an egg and ham casserole, hash browns, cinnamon rolls and orange juice inside the cabin. It's your decision where and what you want to eat."

🍽 **NOVEMBER 5** 🍽

🕴 Chew–Chew's delight: "At Grandma's and Grandpa's cabin, we can choose to eat *both* breakfasts!"

✚ Please remember to pray for your food twice then!

📖 **H**ebrews 4:12 For the Word of God is living and active. Sharper than any double-edged sword, it penetrates even to dividing soul and joints and marrow; it judges the thoughts and attitudes of the heart.

❓**Question of the day: "What is the attitude of our hearts lately?"**

⛊ "Construction paper comes in a variety of colors and is pretty thick stuff. Please be careful with those scissors, especially if you are going to cut out some fancy patterns with them."

🍽 NOVEMBER 6 🍽

⛊ Izzy Ann's agony: "Papercuts come in one color...red (and they hurt!)"

✚ Never run with scissors, which is probably a rare occurrence!

📖 **Luke 6:31 Do to others as you would have them do to you.**

❓Question of the day: "Ouch?"

🧍 **"Today Great Grandma Buckskin is coming for a visit. If you wish, she will trim your hair for you. She doesn't charge anything, but a 'thank you' would be nice and possibly a hug thrown in."**

🍽 NOVEMBER 7 🍽

🐈 **Fudgy's two cents worth: "What a deal!"**

✚ **Please don't take advantage of anyone who is kind enough to help you out!**

📖 **Ephesians 2:8–9 For it is by Grace you have been saved, through faith – and this not from yourselves, it is the gift of God –not by works, so that no one can boast.**

❓**Question of the day: "Are you saved?"**

👤 **"God Requires All to Confess their sins so we can spend Eternity with Him. GRACE is God giving us something good that we don't deserve."**

🍽 NOVEMBER 8 🍽

👤 **Lanore's gratitude: "Thank you God and Jesus!"**

✚ **May the Grace of God be with you all!**

📖 **James 2:8 If you really keep the royal law found in Scripture, "Love your neighbor as yourself," you are doing right.**

❓<u>**Question of the day: "Do we even know our neighbors these days?"**</u>

🧍 **"Remember children to love your neighbor as yourself. Now please pass the dessert tray around the table after you have helped yourselves to one."**

🍽 NOVEMBER 9 🍽

🐱 **Witty Kitty's angle: "A neighbor does not *only* mean the people that live in houses near you. It can also mean anyone you come in contact with."**

➕ **A step further –it can even mean someone in need across the world from you.**

📖 **P**roverbs 22:6 Train a child in the way he should go, and when he is old he will not turn from it.

❓<u>Question of the day</u>: <u>"Are you training your children?"</u>

🕴 "Grandpa, would you like to play some sports with the grandchildren this afternoon after your nap?"

🍽 NOVEMBER 10 🍽

🕴 Mary Lu's delight: "I like Grandpa's idea of 'sports'! They include: horseshoes, croquet, tether ball, baseball, yard golf, mud volley ball and bronco bustin'. What else would a kid want to have fun?"

✚ A hotdog stand and some good insurance wouldn't hurt!

John 15:13 Greater love has no one than this, that He lay down His Life for His friends.

?Question of the day: "Doesn't this say it all?"

"Today is Veterans' Day. Please do *your* part and thank them for our freedom."

🍽 NOVEMBER 11 🍽

Little Trooper's observation: "Grandpa isn't a veteran, but he kind of looks and walks like he was in a war."

✚ Thank Grandpa anyway. Entertaining six grandchildren for the weekend counts for something!

📖 **John 3:16** For God so loved the world that He gave His one and only Son, so that whoever believes in Him shall not perish but have Eternal Life.

❓**Question of the day: "Are you prepared for Eternal Life?"**

🧍 "The cross is not to be worshipped. Instead, it is a reminder of Jesus's love for us."

🍽 NOVEMBER 12 🍽

🐈 Witty Kitty's tip: "You'll find a few scattered on the cabin's walls and a couple around Grandma's and Grandpa's necks."

✚ Thank you God for giving us Your Son and thank You Jesus for giving Your Life for us!

📖 **Z**echariah 10:8 I will signal for them and gather them in. Surely I will redeem them; they will be as numerous as before.

❓**Question of the day: "Are you receiving a signal from above?"**

👤 **"Okay children...this afternoon Grandpa is going to teach you all how to whistle while I take a little nap for myself."**

🍽 NOVEMBER 13 🍽

👤 **Baby No–No's worry: "Grandma told me to put a cork in it, but I don't know where to find one."**

✚ **Second drawer to the right of the ice box and try to be quiet. Your Grandma needs her rest.**

👤 **(Oh...)**

📖 **D**euteronomy 31:6 "...Be strong and courageous. Do not be afraid or terrified because of them, for the Lord your God goes with you; He will never leave you nor forsake you."

❓Question of the day: "Isn't this an awesome promise?"

🧍 "Once in a while out here in the country, you may see a fireman in the tower over yonder watching for signs of smoke, especially if we are experiencing a drought."

🍽 NOVEMBER 14 🍽

🧍 Kimberella's hunch: "I bet when we have an unusually wet summer, he is up there drying out his socks."

✚ At least get your feet wet by trying to share the Good News, which is the Gospel, to your loved ones. You may tell just the right person who could spread it like a wild fire!

📖 **L**uke 6:38 "...Give, and it will be given to you. A good measure, pressed down, shaken together and running over, will be poured into your lap. For with the measure you use, it will be measured to you."

❓**Question of the day: "How are you measuring up?"**

🧍 "I think that coat pockets are a great place to keep and find items in. The coats hanging on the back porch have been known to contain coins, keys, rocks, rings, gloves, photos, matches and used tissues."

🍽 NOVEMBER 15 🍽

🧍 Chew–Chew's disgust: "Eeeeeeeewwww!"

✚ They are also a great place for your cell phone while visiting someone in person.

📖 **P**roverbs 18:1 An unfriendly man pursues selfish ends; he defies all sound judgment.

❓Question of the day: "Do you know someone like this?"

🧍 "Hey kids! Go grab your hobby horses and we'll all gallop around back into the shed's art room and get to work on our own hobbies."

🍽 NOVEMBER 16 🍽

🐕 Fudgy's question: "Why do the kids always get to do the fun stuff, while I'm on a leash outside?"

✚ Because when the kids all go to school, you get to be with Grandma and Grandpa all day...every day!

🐕 Fudgy's rebuttal: "Where can I sign up to be a kid?"

📖 **Judges 6:19** Gideon went in, prepared a young goat, and from an ephah of flour he made bread without yeast. Putting the meat in a basket and its broth in a pot, he brought them out and offered them to him under the oak.

❓Question of the day: "Do you know how to prepare a goat of any age?"

🚶 "If you catch a cold while staying at our cabin, I'll make you some homemade duck soup."

🍽 NOVEMBER 17 🍽

🚶 Mary Lu's conclusion: "Trust me, it will help you feel better fast, so you can get out of 'Dodge' and back to normal food at home in no time!"

✚ No matter what food you are served at another's house, please be thankful!

📖 **R**evelation 4:11 "You are worthy, our Lord and God, to receive Glory and Honor and Power, for You created all things, and by Your Will they were created and have their being."

❓<u>Question of the day: "What more do we need to know?"</u>

👤 "I finally realized that you can't force someone into doing an art project."

🍽 NOVEMBER 18 🍽

👤 Lanore's memory: "At school this week, our teacher told us what we will be creating. I like it better when Grandma lets *us* decide what we will paint and decorate. The only requirement is that we finish what we started."

✝ God created the whole world and everything in it, so there are plenty of ideas out there for everyone to choose from when it comes to art!

📖 **James 5:9 Don't grumble against each other, brothers, or you will be judged. The Judge is standing at the door!**

❓**Question of the day: "What do we have to grumble about?"**

👤 **"Do you know what the difference is between whining and shining?"**

🍽 NOVEMBER 19 🍽

👤 **Izzy Ann's guess: "One letter?"**

✚ **Correct! Now, please no whining at the Buckskins' cabin and this includes Grandma and Grandpa.**

📖 **1 Thessalonians 4:16–18 For the Lord Himself will come down from Heaven, with a loud command, with the voice of the archangel and with the trumpet call of God, and the dead in Christ will rise first. After that, we who are still alive and are left will be caught up together with them in the clouds to meet the Lord in the air. And so we will be with the Lord Forever. Therefore encourage each other with these words.**

❓**Question of the day: "Are we encouraging others today?"**

👤 **"Look! There goes an elephant with a duck on its back! Over there I see a cat chasing a porcupine! There's a giraffe with a lion's head swimming after a rabbit!"**

🍽 NOVEMBER 20 🍽

👤 **Baby No–No's excitement: "I just love 'Cloud Identification Day' at my grandparents' place!"**

✝ **Look! The clouds are parting and there is Jesus for real! Be ready...that day is coming sooner than later!**

📖 **Psalm 27:14 Wait for the Lord; be strong and take heart and wait for the Lord.**

❓Question of the day: "Are you waiting?"

🧍 "Tree houses can be fun to hang out in. Grandpa has a tree stand that looks like a country bus stop hut for children to wait in on a cold morning."

🍽 NOVEMBER 21 🍽

🧍 Chew–Chew's hope: "I'm waiting for Grandma to pack us a lunch so we can eat it in the hut like we did last year. It's such great fun!"

➕ Good things come to those who wait!

📖 **Genesis 1:2 Now the Earth was formless and empty, darkness was over the surface of the deep, and the Spirit of God was hovering over the waters.**

❓**Question of the day: "Does this sound like the Big Bang theory to you?"**

👤 **"Whether it is high tide, low tide or a rip tide – stay away and let it do its thing."**

🍽 NOVEMBER 22 🍽

👤 **Prince Roderick's relief: "I'm just glad there is no tide in the crick."**

✚ **How come the moon causes great tides in the ocean, but not in creeks? Mystery...**

📖 **Leviticus 13:45** "The person with such an infectious disease must wear torn clothes, let his hair be unkempt, cover the lower part of his face and cry out, 'Unclean! Unclean!'"

❓**Question of the day: "How is your health today?"**

🚶 "If you hear coughing and sneezing inside the cabin, you may want to stay outside for about a week."

🍽️ NOVEMBER 23 🍽️

🚶 Izzy Ann's horror: "Then *I'll* be coughing and sneezing for about a week!"

➕ What goes around, comes around. Don't be a part of the vicious cycle. Please cover your nose and mouth and then wash your hands.

📖 **R**evelation 21:19–21 The foundations of the city walls were decorated with every kind of precious stone. The first foundation was jasper, the second sapphire, the third chalcedony, the fourth emerald, the fifth sardonyx, the sixth carnelian, the seventh chrysolite, the eighth beryl, the ninth topaz, the tenth chrysoprase, the eleventh jacinth, and the twelfth amethyst. The twelve gates were twelve pearls, each gate made of a single pearl. The great street of the city was of pure gold, like transparent glass.

❓Question of the day: "Is your imagination running wild like mine is?"

👤 "At the ole cabin there is not much reason to wear jewelry, but in case you do, I have an antique jewelry box you can store your items in while you sleep."

🍽 NOVEMBER 24 🍽

👤 Lanore's delight: "Grandma's jewelry box is a treasure all by itself!"

✚ In the Book of Revelation, you can find quite a bit of information on what the City will look like.

📖 **Matthew 5:38–39** "You have heard that it was said, 'Eye for eye, and tooth for tooth.' But I tell you, do not resist an evil person. If someone strikes you on the right cheek, turn to him the other also..."

❓**Question of the day: "Are we willing to do this no matter what?"**

🧍 "We have a gumball machine that is conveniently located on the way *out* of the cabin. Grandpa designed it so it will only take a Susan B. Anthony coin."

🍽 NOVEMBER 25 🍽

🧍 Mary Lu's threat: "They better be large gumballs for *that* price!"

✚ Don't make threats that you can't carry out or even ones that you can!

Psalm 107:1 Give thanks to the Lord, for He is good; His love endures Forever.

?Question of the day: "Is our love this powerful?"

"At our place in the sticks, Thanksgiving Day is a little bit different. Instead of turkey being the main attraction, it is Spam."

🍽 NOVEMBER 26 🍽

Fudgy's two cents worth: "It's because Prince Roderick needs more hunting time to get a turkey. Swing by for Christmas dinner instead."

✚ Please say 'thank you' to God this Thanksgiving and start saying 'thanks' every time you sit down for a meal. In no time flat you will kick yourself for not doing it sooner!

📖 **A**cts 5:29 Peter and the other apostles replied: "We must obey God rather than men!..."

❓Question of the day: "How does our faith compare to Peter's?"

👤 "I believe that if there is a rule or a law, then there is probably a good reason for it due to past events."

🍽 NOVEMBER 27 🍽

🐱 Witty Kitty's motto: "If Grandma or Grandpa tells me to do something (or *not* to do something), there is a reason. I'm guessing it has something to do with Fudgy."

✚ The sillier the rules or laws are, the more chances it's because someone actually *did* do it at some point.

📖 **1** Peter 3:20 ..."who disobeyed long ago when God waited patiently in the days of Noah while the ark was being built...."

❔**Question of the day: "How much patience do we have while waiting in traffic for more than five minutes?"**

👤 "At our cabin, we have a family tree painted on the wall, which stems back all the way to Noah."

🍽 NOVEMBER 28 🍽

🖊 Little Trooper's question: "Shouldn't it go all the way back to Adam?"

➕ Yes, but the paperwork got kind of wet.

James 1:5 If any of you lacks wisdom, he should ask God, who gives generously to all without finding fault, and it will be given to him.

?<u>Question of the day</u>: "<u>Have you ever asked God for wisdom?</u>"

👤 "Hopefully, my children, your ability to separate make-believe from reality will never leave you."

🍴 NOVEMBER 29 🍴

👤 Kimberella's plan: "I like to keep in God's Holy Word and ask the Holy Spirit to help me remember what it says."

✚ Also to pray for wisdom!

📖 **M**icah 7:17 **They will lick dust like a snake, like creatures that crawl on the ground. They will come trembling out of their dens; they will turn in fear to the Lord our God and will be afraid of you.**

❓**Question of the day: "Do you fear the Lord your God?"**

👤 **"I'm so glad that Grandpa hung up a rope swing on that old hickory tree in our side yard. Watch out for bees, spiders and mosquitoes who like to hang in the water that collected in the tire!"**

🍴 NOVEMBER 30 🍴

👤 **Mary Lu's warning: "And snakes!"**

✚ **Even snakes like to have fun once in a while.**

📖 **E**phesians 6:14–15 Stand firm then, with the belt of truth buckled around your waist, with the breast plate of righteousness in place, and with your feet fitted with the readiness that comes from the Gospel of peace.

❓**Question of the day: "Have you read the Gospels of Matthew, Mark, Luke and John?"**

🧍 **"Okay kiddies, please go to the back porch and look in the lost and found pile of shoes to see if any of them belong to you. There are gym, dress, golf, soccer, swimming, wrestling, loafers, saddle, high–heels, sandals and flip–flop shoes."**

🎁 DECEMBER 1 🎁

🐈 **Fudgy's gripe: "All I have are my own padded paws."**

➕ Obviously, the grandchildren only have their own feet to run around in if they keep leaving their shoes on the back porch at every visit.

📖 **Hebrews** 5:13 Anyone who lives on milk, being still an infant, is not acquainted with the teaching about righteousness.

❓**Question of the day: "Are you still on milk or solid food?"**

🧍 "The best time to *bake* cookies is first thing in the morning. The best time to *eat* them is right out of the oven."

🎁 DECEMBER 2 🎁

🧍 Lanore's announcement: "Time for breakfast!"

➕ Remember to use your manners and not be a glutton.

📖 **Matthew 6:27 Who of you by worrying can add a single hour to his life?**

❓**Question of the day: "Well?"**

🧍 "It is candle making day at the Buckskin's cabin. You'll need your apron, goggles, rubber boots and your favorite color of dye."

🎁 DECEMBER 3 🎁

🧍 Chew–Chew's anxiety: "This could be extremely dangerous!"

✚ Worry about nothing and pray about everything. Oh, and stand back!

Philippians 4:8 Finally, brothers, whatever is true, whatever is noble, whatever is right, whatever is pure, whatever is lovely, whatever is admirable – if anything is excellent or praiseworthy – think about such things.

Question of the day: "Are we thinking about these things on this day?"

"Maybe the reason Grandpa and I have a hard time thinking outside the box is due to the fact that as small children we were always told to stay inside the lines."

🎁 DECEMBER 4 🎁

Baby No–No's know: "They have coloring books now for adults to use with very small areas to color."

✚ It sounds like the manufacturers of crayons, colored pencils and markers were doing a lot of thinking outside the box!

📖 **E**phesians 4:29–30: Do not let any unwholesome talk come out of your mouths, but only what is helpful for building others up according to their needs, that it may benefit those who listen. And do not grieve the Holy Spirit of God, with whom you were sealed for the day of redemption.

❓**Question of the day: "What comes out of our mouths?"**

🧍 "Sometimes I don't feel like cooking, so I ask Grandpa if we can go to the Fiddle Sticks County Diner for a hot meal."

🎁 DECEMBER 5 🎁

🐱 Witty Kitty's wit: "The problem is you can't believe a single thing their waiter says."

➕ Only let what is wholesome come out of your mouth!

📖 **Psalm 105:2 Sing to Him, sing praise to Him; tell of all His wonderful acts.**

❓**Question of the day: "Are you singing yet?"**

🚶 "They *say* that the perfect age to teach a child a musical instrument is four years old. This also goes for learning a foreign language."

🎁 DECEMBER 6 🎁

✏ Little Trooper's thought: "That makes sense since music is kind of like a language all by itself."

✝ Music is music. As long as there are no words, everyone who has the ability to hear, hears the same thing. If a four–year–old is playing the music, however, you may not be able to recognize the melody.

📖 **P**salm 119:103 How sweet are Your Words to my taste, sweeter than honey to my mouth!

❓<u>Question of the day: "Is this the way you feel about God's Word?"</u>

👤 Grandma Buckskin's opinion:

<u>D</u>on't
<u>E</u>at
<u>N</u>othin'
<u>T</u>hat
<u>I</u>s
<u>S</u>ugar
<u>T</u>reated

🎁 DECEMBER 7 🎁

🧍 Izzy Ann's conclusion: "Don't I know it!"

✚ Be kind to everyone and keep your appointment with your dentist. You're going to need it, kid!

📖 **Jude 1:18 They said to you, "In the last times there will be scoffers who will follow their own ungodly desires."**

❓Question of the day: "Do you know a scoffer?"

🧍 "God created the universe. Even a little child can figure out whether something is manmade, like the difference between a watch and a stick."

🎁 DECEMBER 8 🎁

🧍 Chew–Chew's comment: "What time is it?"

🧍 "Time to pick up sticks for the campfire tonight."

🧍 "Oh..."

✚ Please don't be stubborn or a scoffer. Believe God's Word – *all* of it!

📖 **Hebrews 4:16 As it is, you boast and brag. All such boasting is evil.**

❓**Question of the day: "Are we boasting about ourselves or being humble?"**

🧍 **"Grandpa's thankfulness":**

<u>M</u>aking
<u>E</u>veryone
<u>R</u>ealize we should
<u>C</u>herish the fact that
<u>Y</u>ou Love Us

🎁 DECEMBER 9 🎁

🧍 Baby No-No's relief: "Thank you God for always being merciful to me and others!"

✝ We deserve the death that Jesus suffered in our place. Thank you Jesus! Thank you God!

📖 **H**ebrews 7:25 Therefore He is able to save completely those who come to God through Him, because He always lives to intercede for them.

❓Question of the day: "Have you accepted Jesus Christ as your Savior?"

🧍 "Grandpa let Mary Lu drive the go-cart around the acreage yesterday. We heard a blood-curdling scream come from our granddaughter that made our hearts sink. As it turned out, she was stuck in some mud, not wrapped around a tree."

🎁 DECEMBER 10 🎁

🧍 Mary Lu's apology: "I'm sorry you thought I was badly injured. I'll do better the next time I scream. I will practice in my own back yard."

✝ There is a scream for "Help me...I'm stuck!" And "Call 9-1-1!" Thank you God for watching over her. Now where *are* my earplugs?

📖 **Proverbs 19:9 A false witness will not go unpunished, and he who pours out lies will perish.**

❓**Question of the day: "Isn't being truthful much easier and less stressful?"**

🧍 **"Everyone repeat after me, please: 'Do not lie...Do not lie...Do not lie!' At our cabin we have a *'think about that chair'* placed in a corner."**

🎁 DECEMBER 11 🎁

🐈 **Witty Kitty's meow: "That's *not* a lie."**

➕ **One lie usually leads into another lie and then you are *really* going to be in hot water!**

📖 **E**phesians 5:15–16 Be very careful, then, how you live – not as unwise but as wise, making the most of every opportunity, because the days are evil.

❓**Question of the day: "Are you trying to make the most out of every opportunity?"**

🧍 "Today I will teach you all about telling what time it is, so you won't be late for mealtimes anymore. When the big hand is on the 12 and the little hand is on the 9, it is breakfast. When the big and little hands are on the 12 at the same time, it is lunchtime. When the big hand is on the 12 and the little hand is on the 5, it's time to call the pizza joint."

🎁 DECEMBER 12 🎁

🧍 Baby No–No's question: "Why can't we just go ring the dinner bell that's mounted on the back deck?"

✚ Because Grandpa's big hand rang the bell so hard last week, the clapper fell out and dinged Grandma's little hand. Luckily, it wasn't her dialing hand!

📖 **H**ebrews 10:25 Let us not give up meeting together, as some are in the habit of doing, but let us encourage one another – and all the more as you see the Day approaching.

❓<u>Question of the day: "Are we being social in these last days?"</u>

👤 "In a basket of mittens, a pair of red ones will stand out. No matter what color *your* mittens are on your hands, the thumb always stands out. Why is that?"

🎁 DECEMBER 13 🎁

👤 Lanore's feeling: "I wish my thumbs were fingers and then they could be warmed by the other ones."

➕ If we all try to do our own thing, we will end up being all thumbs. God wants us to congregate with each other.

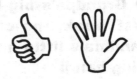

📖 **P**salm 32:8 I will instruct you and teach you in the way you should go; I will councel you and watch over you.

❓<u>Question of the day: "Are you willing to be taught?"</u>

👤 "At our cabin you won't see the police, because they do their paroling in the city. You will see an occasional deputy, however."

🎁 DECEMBER 14 🎁

👤 Izzy Ann's pledge: "Not at Grandma's and Grandpa's place....*never*!"

✚ Never say 'never', but *always* pray for safety and guidance!

📖 Isaiah 31:5 "...Like birds hovering overhead, the Lord Almighty will shield Jerusalem; He will shield it and deliver it, He will 'pass over' it and will rescue it."

❓Question of the day: "Isn't this comforting?"

👤 "Whenever you kiddies cross the road to check our mailbox, please watch out for cars, pickup trucks, school buses, milk trucks, farm machinery, deer, cows, sheep, pigs and geese."

🎁 DECEMBER 15 🎁

👤 Prince Roderick's humor: "Honk, honk!"

✝ Geese are very lucky that God created them with a migration device built in. They know exactly when to fly south for the winter and then return to enjoy the warmth up north. Unlike some snow birds we know.

📖 **P**roverbs 31:21 When it snows, she has no fear for her household; for all of them are clothed in scarlet.

?Question of the day: "Are you prepared for the winter?"

👤 "I'm assuming that it is safe to say that in the southern United State, no child owns a pair of snow pants. For that matter, adults probably don't own any either."

🎁 DECEMBER 16 🎁

💊 Little Trooper's invitation: "That's okay! We have plenty to go around, so please come up and see us some time to play in the snow with us!"

✚ Hospitality at its finest!

Psalm 150:1–6 Praise the Lord. Praise God in His Sanctuary; praise Him in His Mighty Heavens. Praise Him for His acts of Power; praise Him for His surpassing Greatness. Praise Him with the sounding of the trumpets, praise Him with the harp and lyre, praise Him with tambourine and dancing, praise Him with the strings and flute, praise Him with the clash of cymbals, praise Him with resounding cymbals. Let everything that has breath praise the Lord. Praise the Lord.

?Question of the day: "Are you praising Him?"

"Music at our cabin is so much fun! You can pick up an instrument of your choice and play and sing along, dance or just lay back on a bean bag chair by the fireplace and enjoy."

🎁 DECEMBER 17 🎁

Baby No–No's opinion: "Easier said than done."

✚ Music is a wonderful way to share time with your family and friends, as long as you all share the same key with each other before you start!

📖 **E**cclesiastes 3:4 ...a time to weep and a time to laugh, a time to mourn and a time to dance,...

❓Question of the day: "Do you want to laugh and dance with me?"

🧍 "Why is it that tickling seems to be more entertaining for the tickler than the ticklee? The one getting tickled *sounds* like they are having fun, but the tickler is actually the one who gets tickled the most in the end."

🎁 DECEMBER 18 🎁

🧍 Kimberella's fret: "Did that make *any* sense?"

➕ If you really want to tickle someone, know your limits. At the very least, know theirs!

📖 Isaiah 11:2-3 The Spirit of the Lord will rest on him –the Spirit of wisdom and of understanding, the Spirit of counsel and of power, the Spirit of knowledge and of the fear of the Lord –and he will delight in the fear of the Lord.

❓Question of the day: "Do you delight in the fear of the Lord?"

👤 "Stringing popcorn is an old tradition that we would like to pass on to our grandchildren this Christmas season."

🎁 DECEMBER 19 🎁

👤 Izzy Ann's idea: "Can we make a batch of Jiffy Pop for us to eat *before* we get started? Otherwise, I'm afraid that we could end up eating all the other popcorn."

➕ If an idea just pops up into your head, make sure that it is of the Holy Spirit *before* you proceed!

📖 **E**xodus 23:8 "Do not accept a bribe, for a bribe blinds those who see and twists the words of the righteous..."

❓<u>Question of the day: "Have you ever been bribed?"</u>

🧍 "Grandpa told me that he used a long-handled implement to hoist the heavy white stuff that fell from the sky this afternoon."

🎁 DECEMBER 20 🎁

🧍 Mary Lu's cyphering: "He only said it that way so that he can get a bigger piece of cake to go along with his thermos of piping hot cocoa."

✚ Work it!

📖 **S**ong of Solomon 2:11-12 See! The winter is past; the rains are over and gone. Flowers appear on the Earth; the season of singing has come, the cooing of doves is heard in our land.

❓**Question of the day: "Can we say, 'Yeah!'?"**

👤 **"Winter can be very harsh *or* surprisingly kind. Snow skiing, snow days, snow pants, snow angels, ice skating and ice fishing. Brrrr!"**

🎁 DECEMBER 21 🎁

👤 **Izzy Ann's plea: "I need some more hot coca and another blanket for my bed, please!"**

✚ **If we didn't have winter, we wouldn't appreciate Spring.**

📖 **G**enesis 6:17 I am going to bring floodwaters on the Earth to destroy all life under the heavens, every creature that has the breath of life in it. Everything on Earth will perish.

❓Question of the day: "Any questions?"

👤 "There may not be any dinosaur bones in this area surrounding our cabin, however, there are some in other parts of the United States."

🎁 DECEMBER 22 🎁

👤 Chew–Chew's schooling: "They were killed in the flood of Noah's day, but not all of them were. Some are still swimming in over seventy lakes around the world."

✚ We get our oil not only from dead dinosaurs, but other animals and people as well....that's right....people! Would you like Ethanol or Ethel?

📖 **P**roverbs 15:13 A happy heart makes the face cheerful, but heartache crushes the spirit.

❓**Question of the day: "How is your spirit lately?"**

🧍 "Kids, let's hang up our stockings over the fireplace. Mary Lu, Izzy Ann, Lanore, Chew-Chew, Baby No-No, Little Trooper, Prince Roderick and Kimberella."

🎁 DECEMBER 23 🎁

🐕 Fudgy's secret: "Grandma's stocking is the biggest one so she can reach in without taking off her oven mitt while baking us cinnamon rolls."

➕ God created our teeth to be able to chew our food, talk and smile. Don't be in a rush to rot them out on sweets!

📖 **Luke 16:13 "No servant can serve two masters. Either he will hate the one and love the other, or he will be devoted to the one and despise the other. You cannot serve both God and Money."**

❓**Question of the day: "Who do you serve?"**

👤 **"The only *good* thing about wrapping presents is that you actually went shopping so there are presents *to* wrap."**

🎁 DECEMBER 24 🎁

🐱 **Witty Kitty's relief: "I am so glad that Grandma and Grandpa aren't into wrapping fake gifts to place under the Christmas tree and hang on the walls."**

✚ **Now *there* is someone who has too much time on their hands, but it's better than running in the streets.**

📖 **1** Timothy 2:5–6 **For there is one God and one Mediator between God and men, the man Christ Jesus, who gave Himself as a ransom for all men – the testimony given in its proper time.**

?<u>Question of the day: "Did you thank Jesus this morning when you arose from bed?"</u>

👤 **"Today is the birthday of Christ Jesus. Please remember that it is not all about a little baby. He was always living and came down from Heaven as the Son of God in a human body."**

🎁 DECEMBER 25 🎁

🔖 **Little Trooper's reminder: "Please don't use an "X" to replace Christ's Name."**

✝ **MERRY *CHRIST*MAS!**

📖 **M**atthew 15:11 "...What goes into a man's mouth does not make him 'unclean', but what comes out of his mouth, that is what makes him 'unclean'."

❓Question of the day: "What is coming out of our mouths?"

🚹 "We are going to have a 'Food on a Stick' party in a few days. Please bring one of the following food items on a stick: mini hotdogs, fruit, vegetables, cheese, sausage, steak, shrimp, fudge, etc."

🎁 DECEMBER 26 🎁

🚹 Prince Roderick's suggestion: "How about banana cream pie?"

✚ Probably not.

📖 **1** **Peter 5:5 Young men, in the same way be submissive to those who are older. All of you, clothe yourselves with humility toward one another because, "God opposes the proud but gives grace to the humble."**

❓**Question of the day: "Are we practicing humility?"**

🧍 **"What is the difference between a toy box and a garbage can?**

🎁 DECEMBER 27 🎁

🧍 **Baby No–No's answer: "A few steps... if Grandpa trips over something that he told us to pick up and put away – it will be gone!"**

✚ **Listen and respect your elders at *all* times...today, tomorrow *and* yesterday!**

📖 **Job 8:8–10** "Ask the former generations and find out what their fathers learned, for we were born only yesterday and know nothing, and our days on Earth are but a shadow. Will they not instruct you and tell you? Will they not bring forth words from their understanding?…"

❓**Question of the day: "Have you ever asked your older relatives about what they have learned over the years?"**

🧍 "What is the difference between downtown and uptown? Answer: Years and years!"

🎁 DECEMBER 28 🎁

🧍 Izzy Ann's delight: "After the long ride into the city, it's fun to walk around on the sidewalks and shop at the old stores *and* the new!"

✚ A lot can be learned from history. The best book on the subject is the Bible!

📖 **Colossians 3:20 Children, obey your parents in everything, for this pleases the Lord.**

❓**Question of the day: "Are you pleasing the Lord?"**

👤 **"Attention all backpackers (a.k.a. kids twelve and under coming to stay for a while at the Buckskins' cabin)! You are welcome to bring your totes inside, however, please don't put them in the kitchenette where I will trip over them."**

🎁 DECEMBER 29 🎁

👤 **Prince Roderick's lecture: "Also, do *not* place them in front of the fireplace...ouch!"**

➕ **Please don't forget to pack consideration, manners and a treat for your hosts. Thank you!**

📖 **Ephesians 2:10 For we are God's workmanship, created in Christ Jesus to do good works, which God prepared in advance for us to do.**

❓**Question of the day: "Isn't this neat that God prepared in us ahead of time to do certain things?"**

🧍 **"Grandpa is getting out the wagon for anyone who can't walk to the mail box."**

🎁 DECEMBER 30 🎁

🧍 **Chew–Chew's complaint: "If Grandma and those other kids ten years and over would get out of here, we would go faster."**

✝ **Do not be lazy – live your life for Christ so that you can be the hands and feet of Jesus to help out mankind!**

📖 **2 Corinthians 5:17 Therefore, if anyone is in Christ, he is a new creation; the old has gone, the new has come!**

❓**Question of the day: "Are you a new creation yet?"**

🧍 "Hey everybody, let's ring in the New Year. We will wait until midnight rolls around and then Grandpa will throw the basketball off of the roof. We can have soda and cake, blow some whistles and then wake up tomorrow to a brand new year and wait another 364 days to do it all over again!"

🎁 DECEMBER 31 🎁

🧍 Lanore's confusion: "Don't we do these things *every* time we stay over at your cabin?"

✚ Happy New Year to everyone and please make this year count!

Printed in the United States
by Baker & Taylor Publisher Services